STEFFEN HARTMANN, born in 1976 in Freiburg im Breisgau, studied piano in Hamburg and participated as accompanist in master classes with Elisabeth Schwarzkopf and Dietrich Fischer-Dieskau, and has worked closely with the soprano Marret Winger. In 2007, he founded the MenschMusik Institute in Hamburg together with Matthias Bölts, a leading innovator in the field of contemporary music education. He has followed an inner meditative path based on anthroposophy since 1997 and has worked as a teacher of meditation for several years. Steffen Hartmann regularly writes essays on salient topics connected to anthroposophical spiritual science, meditation and music. Together with Torben Maiwald, he founded the publishing house Edition Widar. He has led the Rudolf Steiner Haus Hamburg branch of the Anthroposophical Society since 2012. He is also the author of many books, holds lectures and conducts seminars and concert activities worldwide.

By the same author:

The Michael Prophecy and the Years 2012-2033, Rudolf Steiner and the Culmination of Anthroposophy, 2020

Wege zum Geist, Zum Lebenswerk von Anton Kimpfler, 2012
Von der Philosophie zur Anthroposophie, 2013
Aus Widars Wirken (Co-Editor), 2014
Geistesgegenwart und Schöpferkraft (together with Anton Kimpfler), 2015
Die Michael-Prophetie Rudolf Steiners und die Jahre 2012 bis 2033, 2017
Vom Schicksal der Töne in unserer Zeit, 2018
Benjamin oder das Kind über den Wolken, 2019
Mit Widar Zukunft schaffen (together with Volker Fintelmann), 2019
Einstehen für die Zukunft—mit Michael und Widar, (Co-Editor), 2020
Engel denken. Ein Erkenntnisweg, 2021
Gilgamesch und Enkidu—eine weltgeschichtliche Freundschaft. Eine karmische Studie zu Rudolf Steiner und Ita Wegman, 2021
Auf der Suche nach dem Ich (together with Volker Fintelmann), 2024

ANGEL THINKING

Consciousness, Meditation and Human Destiny

Steffen Hartmann

Translated by Fabian Lochner

TEMPLE LODGE

Temple Lodge Publishing Ltd.
Hillside House, The Square
Forest Row, RH18 5ES

www.templelodge.com

First published in English by Temple Lodge in 2025

Originally published in German under the title *Engel denken,
Ein Erkenntnisweg* by Edition Widar, Hamburg, in 2021

A CIP catalogue record for this book is available from the British
Library

ISBN 978 1 915776 29 7

Cover by Morgan Creative featuring 'Anschauung' by Johannes Greiner
Typeset by Symbiosys Technologies, Visakhapatnam, India
Printed and bound by 4Edge Ltd., Essex

Contents

Foreword

A friend told me about a book she was reading, by Steffen Hartmann. There was 'so much light in his writing,' she exclaimed enthusiastically. My friend is a teacher and curative eurythmist. Her comment made me wonder: How do you write books with 'much light' in them?

I first met Steffen Hartmann in 2011. Before our meeting I had already read a few of his articles. They were written in such a way that I imagined the author to be rather old, serious and wise. The person I met, however, was younger than myself, warm and dynamic. As I got to know Steffen better I observed how quickly he is able to absorb and process thoughts. We started lecturing together. His presentations were always a great deal more succinct than mine. Steffen is gifted with an unusual degree of inner clarity. He never appears to struggle at all to conceive thoughts and put them into words. Time and again I noticed what my friend the eurythmist had pointed out about Steffen: a light-filled way of thinking. Things that others might express awkwardly or struggle to express emerge from his words with ease and transparency. It is this light that makes Steffen a true thinker.

Steffen's first book, however, was not about his own thoughts but rather an effort to shine a light onto someone else's thoughts. *Wege zum Geist. Zum Lebenswerk von Anton Kimpfler* ('Paths towards the Spirit. Anton Kimpfler and his life's work', not translated) was the first of over forty titles from Edition Widar, the publishing house which Steffen founded in 2012 and is still running jointly with a fellow musician, Torben Maiwald. Just as the light at dawn shines on all things and not on itself, Steffen Hartmann let his own first light illuminate the legacy of another.

The fourth title released by Edition Widar was *Von der Philosophie zur Anthroposophie* ('From Philosophy to Anthroposophy', not translated)—a book that has shed new light on the efforts of many thinkers. Some chapters of this book had already been published in the form of articles. They explore the works of different philosophers and various philosophical themes within anthroposophy. In these pages, Steffen brings much clarity to a range of issues which previous writers had failed to elucidate (Carl Unger, Herbert Witzenmann and Sergei O. Prokofieff, among others). This is just the kind of writing that had made me think of its author as a wise old man. *Von der Philosophie zur Anthroposophie* relates to a later work of Steffen's, *Die Michael-Prophetie Rudolf Steiners (The Michael Prophecy and the Years 2012-2033. Rudolf Steiner and the Culmination of Anthroposophy,* Temple Lodge Publishing, 2020) in a way that parallels the relation between Rudolf Steiner's philosophical writings from the nineteenth century and his anthroposophical works in the twentieth century.

Next came *Aus Widars Wirken* ('Widar and his works', not translated), co-edited by Steffen Hartmann, Torben Maiwald and Anton Kimpfler. Widar is the spirit after whom Steffen's publishing company was named. Following the precedent set by Ita Wegman and Nora Stein von Baditz in *Aus Michaels Wirken* ('Michael and his works', German edition: Stuttgart, 1959), Hartmann, Maiwald and Kimpfler gathered together a variety of texts that bear witness to the workings of Widar. Thus they shed light on a spiritual being of great significance for the survival of the earth and of humanity but who until now has remained relatively obscure.

After bringing Anton Kimpfler's ideas into the light and after the collaborative effort of the *Widar* collection it was time for Edition Widar to turn to contemporary issues and questions about the future. Steffen and Anton Kimpfler put their lights together and co-authored *Geistesgegenwart und Schöpferkraft* ('Spirit Presence and Creative Power', not translated), a book that looks at today's challenges in the light of Michael and focuses on Michael in the light of anthroposophically enlivened thinking.

Steffen's next project followed quite organically: *Die Michael-Prophetie Rudolf Steiners und die Jahre 2012-2033 (The Michael Prophecy and the Years 2012-2033. Rudolf Steiner and the*

Culmination of Anthroposophy, Temple Lodge Publishing, 2020). This book deals with the end of the last century and asks whether Rudolf Steiner's prophecies for that time might in fact still lie ahead. Indeed, Steiner worked with a calendar beginning not in the year 1 AD but the year 33 AD—which suggests that the turn of the century and the beginning of the new millennium might actually not happen until 2033. Steffen explores how the much anticipated collaboration between Platonists and Aristotelians might come about at that time and what this could entail for those individuals who had worked with Rudolf Steiner in the early decades of the twentieth century but reincarnated quickly in order to further his work. A very fearless anthroposophical book and no mistake!

We tend to associate light with the sense of sight, and hearing and seeing are generally conceived as polarities. Yet in music there appears to be a form of audible light. The way great composers such as Bach, Mozart, Beethoven, Schubert, Liszt, Wagner, Rachmaninov, Pärt and others shape their melodies; the way their musical themes follow upon one another; and the manner in which the overall structure of a piece of music is designed: all this is comparable to the skilful shaping and combining of light-filled thoughts. The more we can follow what is happening in a piece of music, the better we are able to connect the feeling-thinking we experience when listening to musical melodies with the experience we have when we create our own thoughts. Certainly, the light contained in Steffen Hartmann's books can be explained in part by his being a musician. His little volume on music, *Vom Schicksal der Töne in unserer Zeit* ('The destiny of tones in our times,' not translated) helps musicians and amateurs alike to better understand the tension in contemporary music where we find ourselves suspended, as it were, between the sounds of heaven and the infernal din of sub-sensory electronics.

Since 2011 a close friendship has blossomed between Steffen Hartmann, Torben Maiwald and myself, nurtured by shared study tours and field trips. One day we conceived the project of co-authoring a trilogy on the subject of the Inner Child. In *Benjamin oder Das Kind über den Wolken* ('Benjamin, Child Above the Clouds', not translated) Steffen Hartmann bravely shares personal pre-birth memories of descending into earthly existence. Comparing this poetic, inward little book with *Von der Philosophie zur Anthroposophie* we catch a glimpse of the mystery around Steffen Hartmann's character. Here we have a person who can expound with great authority and learning on the likes of Aristotle, Fichte, Hegel and other great thinkers, who for all that is so deeply in touch with his own inner child that he can listen to intentions and reflections from the sphere of the unborn and speak about them in simple words that touch our hearts. The contrast opens a window into the soul of an anthroposophical musician who is also dedicated to thinking the light. Readers may wish to explore all of Steffen's aforementioned titles in order, listening for the melody of life that sounds in these works, each so different from the other yet all of them united in their kinship with the light.

In *Benjamin* we also hear about the frightful experiences those connected with Michael and anthroposophy had to endure in the spiritual world during the years 1943-1945. In this way, *Benjamin* offers a kind of 'prelude in heaven' to the *Michael-Prophecy* which, in turn, deals with realities and experiences that may await those same souls on the earth, in the years 2012-2033.

Seven years before our first meeting Steffen Hartmann had finished writing *Wesen und Erscheinung. Zugleich ein Versuch, Mensch und Engel zu denken.* ('On Being and Appearance: Exploring the conceptual dimensions of humans and angels'). Selected chapters appeared in the February, March and April issues of the anthroposophical magazine, *Die Drei* (2005). I feel so very pleased that, after repeated encouragements, Steffen Hartmann has finally agreed to publish this book as a whole. Without doubt his style has changed since. Steffen writes more simply now, more directly, more to the point. At that time though, he still adopted the language of philosophy, donning it like a garment one has to wear in order to be taken seriously in certain quarters. Nowadays he speaks more readily by his own lights, from his own heart, and from his own personal experience. At the time, he helped his readers with infinite patience to climb the steps he had laid out so carefully towards those higher regions where thinking and spiritual encounter become one. If we are ready to accept the premise of the book and to follow its pathways inwardly we will receive a very wholesome reward: the thorough cleansing and focusing of our mind. Steffen asks us to really think along and he makes us think hard—but thanks to the author's guiding hand we eventually arrive at our destination: a meeting with angels. We begin to understand how angels think, how humans relate to the angels, and how angels relate to us.

Much of what is written these days about angels is questionable—sometimes tacky, absurd, or in poor taste, often impossible to follow because lacking clarity of thought. Steffen Hartmann's angel book is different. It is an attempt to unite *in thought* with the essence of angels and humans and their relation to one another. That is what makes this little book so valuable in my estimate. In this, Steffen follows a tradition whose greatest exponents are Dionysius Areopagita, Thomas Aquinas and Rudolf Steiner. Indeed, this books appears to me as a masterful tract written by a latter-day pupil of the great Aquinas.

After a long chain of arguments about the thinking of angels the book culminates in two magnificent final chapters, 'On the destiny of thinking and the relation between angels and humans' and 'Meditative epilogue: In conversation with the angels'. The author's ideas about the bonds of mutual responsibility between humans and angels are intensely relevant to our present time. Steffen Hartmann concludes: 'Thus the angels are the destiny of humans and humans become the destiny of angels.' Angels embody our ideals of truth but we humans give meaning to all things (including the deeds of angels) by learning to become free.

In this book, Steffen Hartmann is most insightful and most profoundly spiritual when he speaks about darkness and obstacles.

This concerns the double, sexuality and all those realities that cannot be found through thinking but only by immersing ourselves fully in immediate experience. Here the author reveals links to the path of Christianity. For all its upwards striving, the path of thinking he outlines does not aim for a world of pure and blinding luciferic light. Instead, it aims to understand about mutual responsibility, about the necessity for transforming obstacles, and about the deeper significance of earthly life.

I am grateful that this book is now becoming available to wider circles of readers. When we read it our guardian angels read alongside us. Our thoughts are harmonizing with each other and shine their light together.

Jacob wrestled with an angel. In his dream he saw a heavenly ladder and upon it a multitude of angels rising and descending. May this book be for its readers a ladder of insight—a ladder towards an experience of the angelic world through true understanding.

Angels are messengers of light. In this book the angels themselves are shining their light. They scatter their light in the writings of Steffen Hartmann, in the words of my friend. This book reveals much about the mystery of the light that weaves through Steffen Hartmann's world of thought.

Johannes Greiner

Introduction

There are some questions which, once asked, continue to resound over hundreds or even thousands of years of human history. Such questions are about ultimate meanings. They remain forever alive because they continue to demand answers. An example appears in the following passage from Aristotle's *Metaphysics*:

> We must inquire whether each thing and its essence are the same or different. This is of some use for the inquiry concerning substance; … [I]n the case of so-called self-subsistent things, is a thing necessarily the same as its essence?[1]

Aristotle considers the field of tension between things and concepts, between particular existence and universal ideas, from the point of view of *substance* or *essence*. If we ask about essence or substance in the context of *knowing ourselves* we immediately come up against a kind of boundary or wall: Who am I? What am I? A concrete but mortal individual being? An eternal, immortal being? Perhaps both?

Aristotle is not concerned with psychological self-discovery but with knowledge of our *true being*. Thus the question of our own essential being shifts and turns into a more general question about the nature of truth. This is why Aristotelian science proposes to examine the question of truth in all its dimensions. '…[F]or there is knowledge of each thing only when we know its essence.'[2]

*

In the course of the twentieth century we have witnessed an increasing need for supersensible experience. Some seek out intimate dealings with elemental beings, others probe into their past incarnations, yet others tell of personal encounters with angels or near-death experiences.[3] In this area it is often difficult to distinguish between illusion and reality, particularly when the adopted methods are primarily focused on experience. The risk is that communicating supersensible experience in a research context becomes nigh impossible.

By contrast, there is a tradition, traceable to Aristotle, that seeks to establish *metaphysics* as a proper science. In the early part of the twentieth century, this impulse was taken up by Rudolf Steiner who expanded and developed it into spiritual science or *anthroposophy*. The present study intends to connect with this noetic tradition—in particular with the question: How can philosophical thinking be engaged in building a metaphysics without losing its scientific character by lapsing into blind faith or unreflected spiritual experience?

*

Is it possible at all to build a scientific foundation for a 'metaphysics'? Let us look more closely at one of the ways Aristotle approaches the problem. In the third book of his *Metaphysics*, Aristotle introduces a number of *aporias*, or philosophical puzzles, each containing some seemingly irreducible logical contradictions. Many of these aporias relate to the field of tension between concrete, individual things and generalized concepts or ideas we referred to above. Aristotle introduces his catalogue of puzzles with the following words:

> We must, with a view to the science which we are seeking, first recount the subjects that should be first discussed. ... For those who wish to get clear of difficulties it is advantageous to state the difficulties well; for the subsequent free play of thought implies the solution of the previous difficulties, and it is not possible to untie a knot which one does not know. But the difficulty of our thinking [aporia, *add. SH*] points to a knot in the object; for in so far as our thought is in difficulties, it is in like case with those who are tied up; for in either case it is impossible to go forward. Therefore one should have surveyed all the difficulties beforehand, both for the reasons we have stated and because people

who inquire without first stating the difficulties are like those who do not know where they have to go; besides, a person does not otherwise know even whether he has found what he is looking for or not; for the end is not clear to such a person, while to him who has first discussed the difficulties it is clear.[4]

What Aristotle is saying is that philosophical enquiry is fundamentally about *asking the right questions*. If we accept this approach not just intellectually but by allowing ourselves to experience our questions deep within the soul, then we begin to get a real sense for Aristotle's method in his *Metaphysics*. To allow aporetic thinking—thinking in irreconcilable conceptual contradictions—to become *existential*; to sustain the tension of the paradox; and then to allow metaphysics to arise from the endurance of this tension: such is the pathway of Aristotle's noetic project.

Clearly, it is not of the first importance to have one or the other experience in particular, whether sensory or supersensible. Instead, our *mental instruments* must be sharpened to a point where we can recognize and evaluate supersensible experiences properly, should they occur. Devoted practice of conceptual thinking and an existential relation to its results are the foundation on which to gain knowledge of the metaphysical dimensions of the world.

Aristotle formulated his method during the ancient Greek period of history. At that time, his thoughts did not include the idea of human development. Rudolf Steiner, on the other hand, spearheaded the idea of development according to the conditions that prevailed in his own time, the modern age. In an essay entitled, 'Philosophy and Anthroposophy' (printed in: *Philosophy and Anthroposophy: Collected Essays 1904-1923*, GA 35) Steiner places himself firmly within the Aristotelian philosophical tradition while developing his own original insights concerning the human I (Ego or Self). Indeed, Steiner's particular understanding of the I became the cornerstone of anthroposophy, as we shall explain in more detail in a later chapter ('Angelic encounters and spiritual-scientific investigation').[5]

In our present study we aim to build a new foundation for understanding the I, our essential core, by taking as our starting point the Aristotelian problem of substance or essence. We will argue that the self-awareness of the I in pure thinking is like a needle's eye we must pass through in order to place research into supersensible realities on a solid footing, to be conducted in a way that is healthy and appropriate in a contemporary environment. Moreover, we will try to show how angels—spiritual beings—can play an integral part in our noetic horizon.

Let us acknowledge from the outset that the approach to anthroposophy we are adopting here may well result in certain methodological tensions. In his lecture cycle, *Die geistigen Wesenheiten in den Himmelskörpern und Naturreichen* ('The Spiritual Beings in Celestial Bodies and the Realms of Nature' GA 136), given in Helsinki in April 1912, Rudolf Steiner takes up the question of essences in a most impressive way, ranging from a discussion of elemental beings and the entire hierarchy of angels to the Trinity and the opposing luciferic hierarchies. The cycle opens with a *thinking* approach, as Steiner formulates theoretical principles for knowing angels. As the cycle proceeds, the mode of presentation shifts to concrete descriptions of supersensible facts—descriptions that are based on the highly advanced *clairvoyant perceptions* of the presenter. In this instance, then, Rudolf Steiner addresses the question of essence very much out of the fullness of his own supersensible vision, from which he creates a truly majestic panorama. This lecture cycle is indeed a triumph of spiritual-scientific investigation, on account of the richness of its material, its well thought-out construction, and the admirable clarity of its methodology.

Nonetheless, we may harbour some doubts. We must readily admit that our own capacity for spiritual perception in no way reaches the heights of Rudolf Steiner's. For the sake of scientific probity, then, should we not rather seek *our own thinking capacity* as a starting point? How to turn this dilemma to our advantage? By enriching our thinking with perceptive and emotive faculties, we may have a hope of accessing the sphere of angelic beings ourselves as conscious, mindful individuals, thus overcoming our dilemma step by step.

Let us add one further observation. In this Introduction we have referred several times to the concept of *science*. A proper discussion and definition of this term will be presented in a later chapter, 'The concept of knowledge', which builds on Rudolf Steiner's foundational works on epistemology.

Even at this early stage, however, we may wonder whether in the twenty-first century belief in scientific truth is not hopelessly outdated. Has not the development of science in the previous century brought about the banishment of all absolute claims to truth from scientific discourse? The German philosopher, Gernot Böhme, offers some helpful perspectives on the problem of science in his book, *Am Ende des Baconschen Zeitalters* ('At the End of the Age of Bacon', 1993, not translated). The author offers a summary of the so-called 'consensus' theory of truth, as formulated by the critical theorist, Jürgen Habermas:

> We must assume that at any time in history certain groups of people are tasked with deciding what is to be counted as a true statement in science. … A statement will be considered scientific if it accords with the system of reasoning belonging to a particular scientific community in history. Any statement is considered scientific only when it is operative, i.e. when it has been produced in such a way that its claims are accessible to verification by a scientific community. The norms of science are therefore liable to change, along with the structures of the scientific community itself.[6]

According to Habermas, 'truth' is defined as whatever is capable of generating consensus. Gernot Böhme, however, argues against this position:

> A statement is not true because one reaches, or is able to reach, agreement about it. On the contrary: If we are able to agree on a statement at all, it is because it is true.[7]

Yet even Böhme's counter-argument remains problematic, as scientific communities may also agree on something that is false. Therefore, the mere capacity of reaching agreement is not *of necessity* based on truth.

The background for all consensus-based theories about truth is the philosophy of Karl Popper which underpins much of twentieth-century theory of science. Gernot Böhme summarizes this as follows:

> All scientific knowledge, according to Popper, is 'conjectural' or 'hypothetical knowledge'. Scientific work consists in improving hypotheses in view of making them 'approaching' the truth more and more closely. Accordingly, in Popper's view, the search for truth is a matter of *gradually approximating* truth.[8]

Popper's views on science are referred to as 'falsificationism', the position according to which all scientific knowledge must be, *in principle*, disprovable (that is, falsifiable). According to Popper, therefore, any avoidance of a fundamental openness to falsification is to be judged pseudo-scientific. This widely influential theory is disputed quite emphatically by Gernot Böhme:

> The concepts of 'conjecture' and 'approximation of truth' are meaningless if we don't have any idea in the first place of what it might mean to reach the truth eventually, or even, for that matter, to hit upon it by chance—that is, if we don't already possess at least some criteria that allows us to judge whether what we have before us is true. ... Any evolutionary theory of knowledge that conceives of knowledge as a kind of 'adaptation' has nothing whatever to do with truth.[9]

The fact that a respected contemporary philosopher dares to stake a claim for the idea of scientific truth gives the author of *this* study the courage to frame the problem of substance and essences likewise as a question of truth, and to support his own claims to truth by means of a fully-fledged theory of knowledge inspired by the work of Rudolf Steiner.

1. On the category of substance

In the pages that follow we shall look at a classic pair of opposites, *substance* and *appearance*. Our primary focus will be on certain conceptual linkages that emerge when questions about substance and appearance are raised. The background for our investigations are the teachings of Plato and Aristotle regarding the concept of substance.

The concept of *substance* or *essence* [German: *Wesen*] always implies that of *being* or *existence* [German: *Sein*]. Any substance must possess being of one kind or another. Being can be further differentiated into living and lifeless being. When life is present we call it a living being [German: *Lebewesen*]. On earth, living beings belong to one of three kingdoms: the plant kingdom, the animal kingdom, and the human kingdom. By contrast, the mineral kingdom manifests lifeless being.

We can only speak of *a* being if this being has an identity—that is, if it distinguishes itself from all others as a unique and singular being, a clear and identifiable unit. We may ask by what criteria we recognize the identity of a being. Here, the definition of substances given by Aristotle (384-322 BC), along with various subcategories, can prove helpful. They are found in the *Categories*, one of Aristotles' most famous texts:

> A *substance*—that which is called a substance most strictly, primarily, and most of all—is that which is neither said of a subject [substrate] nor in a subject [substrate], e.g. the individual man or the individual horse. The species in which the things primarily called substances are, are called *secondary substances*, as also are the genera of these species. For example, the individual man belongs in a species, man, and animal is a genus of the species; so these—both man and animal—are called secondary substances.[10]

In this passage Aristotle defines substance as that which does not appear 'in a subject', that is, the underlying ground or *substrate*, but rather in a singular, unique being. He gives the example of an individual man. Aristotle is saying that *individuals themselves* are the underlying ground or substrate from which all specific determinations arise. Significantly, Aristotle ranks the more abstract concepts of *species* ('man' or 'human') and *genus* ('animal' or 'living being') only as 'secondary substances'. The differentiation of substances and their hierarchic ranking into 'primary' and 'secondary' is emphasized even more strongly further on:

> Thus all the other things are either said of the primary substances as subjects [substrates] or in them as subjects [substrates]. So if the primary substances did not exist it would be impossible for any the other things to exist.[11]

Thus Aristotle accords absolute priority to the first order of substances, that is, to the unique, flesh-and-blood, individual beings we see before us. This position is in sharp contrast with the Platonic view that *ideas* are the true substance of things. In order to avoid misunderstandings and one-sidedness in our arguments we must always keep in mind this particular tension between Plato and Aristotle regarding the concept of substance.

In the following passage, Aristotle enters more deeply into the relation between concrete individual beings ('primary substances') and their *species* and *genera* ('secondary substances'):

> Every substance seems to signify a certain 'this'. As regards the primary substances, it is indisputably true that each of them signifies a certain 'this'; for the thing revealed is individual and numerically one. But as regards the secondary substances, though it appears from the form of the name—when one speaks of man or animal—that a secondary substance likewise signifies a certain 'this', this is not really true; rather, it signifies a certain qualification—for the subject [substrate] is not, as the primary substance is, one, but man and animal are said of many things. However, it does not signify simply a certain qualification as white does. White signifies nothing but a qualification, whereas the species and the genus mark off the qualification of the substance—they signify substance of a certain qualification.[12]

Thus, according to Aristotle, substances of the second order—or if you will, the ideas of *species* and *genus*—are much more closely related to the first substances (the individual) than other types of qualities, such as the colour white.

2. On substance and appearance

From a Platonic point of view it must be assumed that any substance or essence is *in principle* able to appear, i.e. to manifest in the sense world, even though it is of purely spiritual origin. In his dialogue, *The Republic*, Plato (427-347 BC) writes about the relationship between the manifold world of appearances and the unified world of ideas:

> And in respect of the just and the unjust, the good and the bad, and all the ideas or forms, the same statement holds, that in itself each is one, but that by virtue of their communion with actions and bodies and with one another they present themselves everywhere, each as a multiplicity of aspects.[13]

And a little further on:

> We predicate 'to be' of many beautiful things and many good things, saying of them severally that they are, and so define them in our speech. ... And again we speak of a self-beautiful and of a good that is only and merely good, and so, in the case of all the things that we then posited as many, we turn about and posit each as a single idea or aspect, assuming it to be a unity and call it that which really is. ... And the one class of things we say can be seen but not thought, while the ideas can be thought and not seen.[14]

According to Plato's worldview those things that are manifest are visible but cannot be grasped by the mind. On the other hand, the substances or essences that *underlie* all appearances belong to the world of *ideas* which cannot be seen with physical eyes but are beheld and understood by the mind only.

Every being manifests under different conditions. All plants, such as beech trees—or rather the *species* of beeches—require the presence of the four elements in order to become perceptible to our senses: earth, water, air, as well as light and warmth. Only the presence of these elements will allow a beech tree to manifest in the earthly realm. If the proper conditions are fulfilled, then a particular specimen of the species 'beech' can grow.

Manifest beings inhabit space and time. The various shapes and forms of plants unfold in a temporal sequence. Individual forms may appear and disappear but their underlying essence remains the same. That is the nature of all essential beings: they are lasting and undying. Certainly, earthly conditions themselves may sometimes be adverse to the growth of beech trees. If the entire planet were contaminated with radioactivity not a single beech tree would be able to live, grow or manifest. But the essence of the beech tree—in the Platonic sense, which comprises all possible beech trees, past, present and future—would not thereby disappear.[15] Such an essential being [German: *ein Wesenhaftes*], which appears in the earthly realm to imprint and express itself there, is a substance founded entirely *in itself*. It is only because of the special nature of this substance that we are able to gather in a single focal point in our mind the many diverse forms of its appearance.

3. On being and becoming

We have learned that the manifestation of being implies becoming, development in time. We can distinguish three levels of development: the development of life (growth), soul development (moral maturation) and spiritual development (the building of capacities). In human beings all three levels are closely interconnected and integrated. The life of the soul requires a living organism as its foundation while spirit manifests within the soul.

The idea of becoming is an area where Plato and Aristotle are more closely aligned. Both thinkers believe that human beings are capable of change. Aristotle puts it this way:

> It seems most distinctive of substance that what is numerically one and the same is able to receive contraries. In no other case could one bring forward anything, numerically one, which is able to receive contraries. For example, a colour which is numerically one and the same will not be black and white, nor will numerically one and the same action be bad and good; and similarly with everything else that is not substance. A substance however, numerically one and the same, is able to receive contraries. For example, an individual person—one and the same—becomes pale at one time and dark at another, and hot and cold, and bad and good.[16]

Plato, in his famous simile of the cave, describes the development of the soul as follows:

> But our present argument indicates, said I, that the true analogy for this indwelling power in the soul and the instrument whereby each of us apprehends is that of an eye that could not be converted to the light from the darkness except by turning the whole body. Even so this organ of knowledge must be turned around from the world of becoming together with the entire soul…until the soul is able to endure the contemplation of essence and the brightest region of being. And this, we say, is the good, do we not?[17]

Admittedly, the two thinkers are making their argument quite differently. Aristotle uses everyday, concrete examples, while Plato is concerned with the soul's inner, esoteric training. Plato links the knowledge of being (the Platonic ideas) with moral realities ('the good' is called the 'brightest region of being'), while Aristotle examines a peculiar property of the category of substance: being one and identical to itself yet at the same time being able to receive multiple contrasting qualities.

Despite their differences in approach, the idea of development is clearly a shared feature in Platonic and Aristotelian thinking. Each admits that people ('the indwelling power of the soul' according to Plato; 'an individual person' as stated by Aristotle) are able to change and grow.

4. On being and consciousness

We have reached the point in our investigation where the problem of the relationship between being and consciousness must be raised. A being may or may not have awareness of itself. At the same time, different degrees of self-awareness may be observed and experienced by different beings. Thus we can distinguish:

- unconscious beings;
- conscious beings;
- beings with self-consciousness.

Minerals and plants display no appreciable expressions of consciousness—at least in their earthly aspect. In the case of minerals this is emphasized further by their inability to move of themselves. Only some outside agent—a storm or a human hand—can move a stone to make it change its location.

Compared to minerals, plants are a great deal more versatile. Their growth is typically directed upwards, toward the light. However, the direction of growth in the plant kingdom should not necessarily be interpreted as an expression of consciousness. Plants merely respond to the prevalent conditions of growth, according to the nature of their particular kind.

Animals have many ways of expressing their consciousness and their sensory awareness of the world. They certainly belong in the category of conscious beings. Whether animals achieve true awareness of themselves as individuals remains a subject of debate.[18]

By contrast, human beings experience self-awareness of their personhood in almost every aspect of their lives. This is a type of consciousness that is able to refer to itself as 'I' and forms notions of 'mine' and 'thine'. It remains to be seen whether this I-consciousness represents an awareness of one's true being or merely of the form of one's appearance.

Significantly, the question of the nature of consciousness is one that only a self-conscious human being can ask themselves. Self-awareness thus presents us with an unsolved riddle which each individual has the choice to wrestle with for themselves. The problem that poses itself is this: I know I experience myself as a person with a name, a family, a certain age, certain qualities etc.—but *who* is this being that manifests within all these different aspects of my personality? Who am I?

It is a question about the nature of the I—and it is a double question: first, about the human I in general (universally and conceptually, in the Platonic sense); and secondly, about ourselves and our own particular I (concrete and real, according to the Aristotelian perspective).

*

Before we turn to these questions in detail let us summarize what we have learned so far regarding the concept of substance or essential being: substance implies the categories of being, life, and identity. Furthermore, the idea of appearance or manifestation belongs to substance as well because whatever appears or manifests must of necessity be some being or substance. Appearance is differentiated further through the concepts of space, time and development. And finally, the idea of substance inevitably leads to questions about being and consciousness.

5. The I and I-consciousness

I-consciousness implies the ability to ask questions about oneself and one's condition. What did I experience at such and such a time? What do I feel like right now? What do I want to do tomorrow? The I can also ask more general questions about its own nature. The capacity that allows us to ask such questions is our *thinking*. It is from thinking, therefore, that we derive both our self-awareness and the possibility of examining the relationship between self-consciousness and ourselves, our I.

The concept of appearance gives us some provisional insight: everything we encounter in time and space, everything that occupies a particular spot and is shaped in a particular way, is *nothing but appearance*.[19] All appearance is necessarily transient as well as confined within spatial boundaries. This holds true for our own self-manifestations also, and it includes everything within the compass of our ordinary self-consciousness. Bodies change their shape and ultimately pass away. Feelings and perceptions come and go. Awareness of ourselves is snuffed out each time we go to sleep.[20] Here we are reaching some real limits to our self-consciousness. We meet a very definite boundary which appears to threaten our very existence. For we may well ask ourselves: Where are we, how are we, and who are we when we have *no consciousness* of ourselves at all?

At this point, if we decide to keep to the realm of appearances we are stymied. We can go no further. And the wall we are facing is raised precisely by our own immersion in the world of appearances. There is only one way forward. We must turn to that which allows us to ask our questions and seek answers for them in the first place: our thinking. First, however, our thinking must be made fit for purpose. It must be cleansed of anything that relates to mere appearance. It must be turned into *pure thinking*. For in pure thinking our inner activity is no longer mediated by space (inner and outer) or by time. We are no longer determined by appearances. Pure thinking is pure in-sight.

6. On pure thinking

Plato describes pure thinking as follows:

> I mean that which the reason itself lays hold of by the power of dialectic, treating its assumptions not as absolute beginnings but literally as hypotheses, underpinnings, footings, and spring-boards so to speak, to enable it to rise to that which requires no assumption and is the starting point of all, and after attaining to that again taking hold of the first dependencies from it, so to proceed downward to the conclusion, making no use whatever of any object of sense but only of pure ideas moving on through ideas to ideas and ending with ideas.[21]

When we think we do not need the help of images to make abstract concepts more concrete. We can operate within the logical structure of concepts and ideas alone. When we do so we have a direct and unmediated experience of pure thinking. Moreover, during the process of thinking we experience ourselves as one with our thoughts. For thoughts arise from our own thinking activity in our own consciousness. Not a single element appears as a *mere given* to our mind. On the contrary, the content of our thoughts is *created* by our own activity. We experience our thoughts as clear, understandable and transparent because we ourselves are involved in shaping them.

It is important to let this reality sink in. In contrast with most experiences of the universe, pure thinking is always, entirely and undeniably comprehensible and transparent *in and of itself*. There is no need to add any external explanations to elucidate it. Let us take as an example the relation between the concepts of *substance* and *appearance*. The concept of appearance actually calls forth the concept of substance or essence *from within itself*, for appearance always implies that something else is manifesting in it. Likewise, if we attribute agency to being, the concept of substance or essence *implies* the concept of appearance (i.e. substance or being expresses itself, becomes manifest). Of course, we could find a great many examples for the connection between substance and appearance.

All of these examples would presuppose a purely conceptual link among them, such as we have described it. What is significant here is that these links are valid and fully understood without needing to refer to any examples at all, simply as a coherent logical nexus.

With this step I believe we have demonstrated that self-consciousness is a kind of *clairvoyance* within the ambit of thinking.[22] By 'thinking clairvoyance' we mean that things that normally remain veiled, as it were, because of their impermanent way of manifesting are becoming transparent and comprehensible. That is precisely what happens in pure thinking.

This insight is central to the argument we are trying to make in this book. Let us follow our reflections a little further and go back for a moment to the philosophy of Aristotle. In his *Metaphysics*, the philosopher formulates one of the fundamental principles of ontology—the first axiom of his *Metaphysics*, as it were:

> There is a principle in things, about which we cannot be deceived, but must always, on the contrary, recognise the truth,—viz. that the same thing cannot at one and the same time be and not be...[23]

When we hold this statement in our mind we have an immediate sense of its self-evident truth. The correctness of the statement that one and the same thing cannot at the same time be and not be is immediately obvious to us the very moment we think it. If we try to describe this experience of self-evidence more exactly we notice something very striking. On the one hand we realize that we are producing this self-evident thought content *ourselves* by means of *our own thinking activity*. On the other hand, in order to experience the sense of self-evidence our thinking must first be *activated* by means of *the thought content itself*. Thus, content and thinking activity form a certain unity *in the act of thinking*.

We can differentiate the unity of content and activity further. Looking at it from the point of view of the *thinker* a thought manifests *within the act of thinking*, i.e. it is mediated by our thinking activity. By choosing a slightly different wording, *through the act of thinking*, we can put more emphasis on the *power* of the thinking activity which generates our individual thoughts.

If, on the other hand, we take the point of view of *content*, the expression *within the act of thinking* indicates that our thinking activity must always appear through the medium of a particular *content* (indeed, thinking with no content is no thinking at all!); while in this context the alternative wording *through the act of thinking* means that our thinking can be activated only in relation to a specific content and its inherent lawfulness.[24] It is as if our thinking 'crystallizes' in response to some perfectly clear and self-determined thought content!

What we see here is a kind of feedback loop between thought content and thinking activity, a movement that originates from both poles of the thinking act equally. To sum up the process: first our thinking reaches for a certain conceptual content. This content, we then discover, is determined by itself. The content reacts back onto our thinking activity which must then proceed with its thinking according to laws that are inherent to the content. The following chart illustrates the act of thinking and its subdivisions as we have developed them:

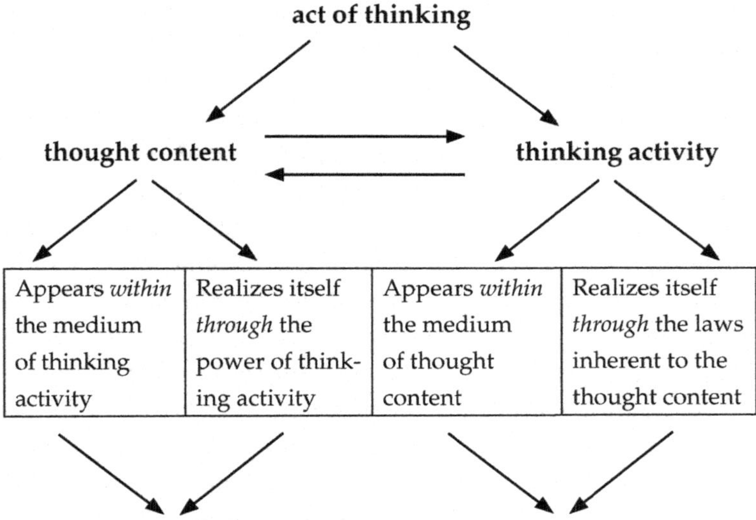

self-evidence, respectively thinking clairvoyance of the thinker

If we allow what is presented in this graphic to arise in us as an inner experience, then the expression *thinking clairvoyance* we used earlier to describe pure thinking will appear quite justified.[25]

Pure thinking, as defined it here, can be developed through general concepts such as substance and appearance, being and non-being etc. All forms of geometrical and mathematical objects are grasped likewise through acts of pure thinking. Geometry and mathematics offer a relatively accessible way for beginners—especially nowadays—to achieve pure thoughts with no sensory input.

Take the idea of a circle. A circle can be defined in different ways, for example as 'the section of a sphere,' or as 'an infinity of points in the same area that are equidistant from a point in that area'. Neither definition is concerned with *individual* circles but only with the law that describes *all* circles. Of course, we mustn't equate the general law of the circle with any of its possible definitions. The same law can be defined in different ways. All particular definitions point to that one law and bring it to expression. The law itself, however, while comprising all of its definitions, remains inexpressible. Every law—such as the law of the circle— constitutes a clear and unalterable mental structure which we, as thinkers, cannot change. We cannot rightfully state: 'A circle is a five-pointed figure in the third dimension.' We may speak those words but they are meaningless and, in fact, impossible to think.

Thus, in pure thinking we encounter a rather paradoxical situation. On the one hand, we are *active* as thinkers, we are creative in the highest degree. Yet, at the same time, we are reduced to merely take note of the content of our thoughts, to *discern* as clearly as possible a reality that is not created by us but determined only by itself.

Obstacles

The practice of pure thinking can provoke a deep sense of malaise in the soul. This malaise is linked to our desire for 'full-blooded life' and our aversion to 'dead thoughts'. The realm of our feelings (our drives and passions, joys and sorrows) and the world of our sensory perceptions seem so much more alive and interesting and real to us than our mental activity.

Aside from the fact that without thinking all our feelings and perceptions would be mere appearances, doomed to remain forever mysterious and incomprehensible, our malaise is justified at least in one respect. When we start practising pure thinking we will inevitably come up against certain limitations. Indeed, pure thinking does not allow the mind to penetrate the concrete reality of beech trees, leopards or thunderclouds *completely*—at least not with the kind of mental clarity that is achieved in mathematics. That is quite impossible. With concrete objects and phenomena there will always remain a significant residual experience which is only accessible to the senses.

There is another kind of limitation too. Within all the wide world of ideas, our mind can only ever focus on one thought at a time. We only have access to isolated fragments of thought, cut from a large and unified mental universe. This begs the question whether instead of continuing to deal with mere fragments we might not imagine a much larger conceptual framework—a framework so comprehensive that it would give us access, in a grounded way, to the *totality* of mental-spiritual life.[26] In the following chapters we shall make such an attempt while further deepening the concept of substance in relation to knowing ourselves and to knowing angels.

7. On thinking and the I

The true nature of the I is deeply connected with the nature of *thinking*. For only through thinking can we hope to gain insight into the I. It is fair to say that the I is *dependent* on thinking for knowing itself. Our individual I and the essence of thinking interpenetrate whenever we turn our mind to anything at all—even when we don't notice. One could say, that when we think we penetrate into the *substance* of thinking. The substance of thinking, in turn, is made manifest (if only partially) through the thinking activity of each individual I. Thinking never imposes itself. On the contrary, it must always be actively willed. Consequently the substance of thinking can only manifest through the freely chosen mental effort made by individual human beings. We have already noted that the *general* question of the nature of the I is related to the status of the *individual* self in the web of human destinies. Likewise, regarding the substance of thinking, we must not stop at general, abstract considerations but search for the real, spiritual, thinking *being* in us that mediates the forming of universal concepts. The fact that the substance of thinking can manifest—at least in principle—in *every* human being suggests that we are looking for a very exalted and all-embracing kind of spirit being.

Walter Johannes Stein (1891-1957) was a thinker who, in the context of his quest for spiritual understanding, went very deeply into these kinds of questions. He writes as follows:

> Whenever I am engaged in thinking, I am not at all this individual human walking on the earth in a physical body. When I think I take part in a fuller, far more extensive kind of being. This was a great puzzle for me in my soul, a puzzle I could not solve. What sort of being could this be? Fortunately, there was an occasion when I could put my question to Rudolf Steiner. His answer was: 'It is a kind of group soul of humanity, the most ancient spirit from the ranks of the Archai who is just now moving on to become a Spirit of Form.'[27]

If we keep following this line of enquiry we will eventually arrive at what medieval theologians such as Dionysius Areopagita (ca. first century AD) and John Scotus Eriugena (ca. 810-877) have described as a realm of hierarchically ordered spiritual beings.[27a] From this perspective, the substance of thinking can be identified quite literally as an angelic being: the 'most ancient from the ranks of the Archai' who is now a 'Spirit of Form' acts, as it were, as a *cosmic bearer of thoughts*. It is this being who makes thoughts available to all human beings as soon as they engage in thinking.

When we prepare to do spiritual-scientific research regarding angels it is vital that we use the *same methods* we followed when we enquired about the self and about the nature of thinking. In principle, our research could extend over a wide range of angelic entities (guardian angels, folk spirits, time spirits, and so forth). For this study we shall limit ourselves to an investigation of those angels that are the closest to us—our guardian angels.

Let us sum up what we have learned about being and consciousness and their relation to each other. Through a cognitive process our being ('this particular person') realizes itself and becomes self-conscious. It is indeed only through cognition that we may become self-aware at all. Therefore, in making thought and ideas accessible to the human I, the Being of Thought is reaching out to us and offering us an element that serves our individual, spiritual self-realization.

What does this process look like? Thinking involves so much more than just having thoughts—if we allow it to become an activity of our I. Thinking is the realization of our I's potential by means of our noetic activity. The thinking I can realize itself *in* and *through* the fabric of its thoughts.

We have now been offered the key to the spiritual development of our individuality. It is our own *search* for answers, our own individual *cognitive activity* alone that has the power to make each of us grow into a real, substantive, empowered and formed self. Experience teaches us that the *potential* for true self-hood is given to us as a *gift*. *Realizing* this potential is a task that belongs to each of us individually. No one can fulfil someone else's calling to become themselves. Thus the spiritual development of each human being is vitally predicated on the element of *freedom*.

8. The concept of knowledge

By now it will be obvious to the reader just how intimately the concept of knowledge is linked to the idea of substance or being.[28] If we try to understand how being acquires self-knowledge we must become clearer about the idea of knowledge itself. Various aspects of the act of cognition have already been touched upon. At this point we wish to elaborate further on the topic by referencing the work of Rudolf Steiner (1861-1925). Rudolf Steiner must be credited as the first thinker who treated the idea of knowledge in a truly comprehensive way. It was his greatest contribution to the history of thought. One might go so far as to say that in Rudolf Steiner's foundational writings (*Outline of a Theory of Knowledge according to Goethe's Worldview*, *Truth and Science* and *The Philosophy of Freedom*) the search for the idea of knowledge, which had been pursued with great intensity for more than two thousand years, has reached its climax and its completion.

This achievement of Rudolf Steiner's remains largely unrecognized. Consequently, it has not been able to bear fruit in the world of mainstream research. A few authors have reflected in some depth on this phenomenon, as well as on Steiner's theory of knowledge. Foremost among them is Hans Erhard Lauer (1899-1979) whose work, *Die Wiedergeburt der Erkenntnis* ('The Rebirth of Knowledge', not translated, German original out of print) was published in 1946. In this book, Lauer describes the principal stages in the historic development of philosophy and science, from ancient Greece and medieval scholasticism to the modern period. He shows how the idea of knowledge progressed despite getting frequently side-tracked through bias and misunderstandings.

Lauer's work leaves no doubt that the *field of tension* between tangible things and universal ideas, perceptions and concepts, being and appearance (discussed in the Introduction) is the true fulcrum on which our *understanding of the process of understanding* hinges.

The critical difference in Rudolf Steiner's theory of cognition is his starting point. Steiner's novel approach is already hinted at in the subtitle of his *Philosophy of Freedom*: 'Soul observations according to the method of natural science.' The *method of natural science* had, of course, been practised and refined since the beginning of the modern period. Steiner proposes to apply this method to the observation of the *human soul*—especially insofar as the soul seeks knowledge and acts according to knowledge. By adopting this approach Steiner revolutionizes the entire field of epistemology, freeing it from the philosophical biases and presumptions of the past.

> What is it that characterises 'scientific' or 'philosophical' knowledge?

That is the key question Hans Erhard Lauer asks in his book.

> [Scientific and philosophical knowledge] are characterised first and foremost by the fact that philosophical knowledge operates mostly with concepts—that is: general ideas—while scientific knowledge takes into account both concepts and percepts, ideas and sense phenomena, in equal measure.[29]

Thus Rudolf Steiner is able to begin his observations of the noetic process without any implicit, presumed theoretical framework. That is what is exciting and unique about his epistemology. His approach allows him to examine the two polarities in the process of cognition, i.e. perception and thinking, in equal measure. This leaves him free to develop an understanding of *both* pure thinking and pure perception.

Rudolf Steiner doesn't just describe the *experience* of thinking. In the third chapter of *The Philosophy of Freedom*, he also develops a systematic understanding of the *observer's consciousness* as directed toward thinking. By refraining from speculation and engaging in direct and unbiased observation of both pure perception and pure thinking, Steiner achieves true presuppositionlessness, a goal that had eluded all those who theorized about cognition before him. Indeed, Steiner refused to front-load his investigation with any preconceived theory, beginning instead with the phenomena of perception as an *immediate given*.

We can become aware of *pure perception* ourselves with the help of a simple experiment. It consists in trying to filter out from our everyday perceptions all those concepts, interpretations and misinterpretations we project onto our experiences of the world. Pursuing this exercise with regularity and discipline we will experience something very peculiar: a jumble of completely indeterminate, chaotic and disjointed impressions. We cannot make out anything specific about this condition beside asserting that it exists. But the experiment demonstrates that unmediated perceptions are utterly unintelligible and disconnected from one another *as long as we rely on perception alone*. The world of pure perception is a complete mystery! Of course, pure perception as such does not normally occur in our everyday consciousness. Our perceptions are usually mixed up with all manner of concepts. So we mostly don't notice how much conceptual interpretation we let slip into our experiences of the world! Experimenting with pure perception brings all this to the surface. It makes us realize to what extent pure perception is a liminal state within the ambit of our consciousness.

Turning now to pure thinking, we recall that this only occurs when we intentionally engage our mind in thinking activity. We may recall from a previous chapter ('On pure thinking') that *thinking activity* is produced entirely by *ourselves* while the *content* of our thoughts is determined entirely by *itself*. The internal logic of our thoughts follows its own laws that do not depend on us. It was Rudolf Steiner's great contribution to show that when a *percept* is brought together with its matching *concept* the problem of cognition is solved satisfactorily. In the complete act of cognition the lawfulness of our thinking brings light and order to the indeterminedness and chaos of our perceptions.

Before examining the idea of knowledge further we would like to introduce our readers to a few authors who, like Hans Erhard Lauer, did grasp the significance of Rudolf Steiner's contribution. Helmut Kiene, in his *Grundlinien einer essentialen Wissenschaftstheorie* ('Outline of an essentialist theory of science', 1984, not translated, German original out of print) elaborates further on Lauer's ideas. Kiene points out significant flaws in the scientific paradigms of David Hume, Immanuel Kant and Karl R. Popper, all of whom remain greatly influential today. Kiene goes on to explain in great detail how the theories proposed by these thinkers have led to certain errors and paradoxes in the modern understanding of science—and how these errors can be corrected with the help of Steiner's epistemology.

Next, we have Walter Johannes Stein's dissertation, *Die moderne naturwissenschaftliche Vorstellungsart und die Weltanschauung Goethes, wie sie Rudolf Steiner vertritt* ('The modern concept of natural science and Goethe's worldview, as advocated by Rudolf Steiner', 1921, not translated), which was written in close collaboration with Rudolf Steiner. Stein's study was, in fact, the very first anthroposophically oriented academic dissertation. It was later published with a learned commentary by Thomas Meyer. A central theme in Walter Johannes Stein's study is the question of higher forms of knowing beyond ordinary consciousness and their theoretical framework—in other words, the question of angelic knowledge. We will develop this theme in a later chapter.

More recently, Renatus Ziegler has published a comprehensive commentary of the *Philosophy of Freedom: Intuition und Ich-Erfahrung* ('Philosophy of Freedom: Intuition and I-experience', Stuttgart 2006, not translated), which he conceived as an independent study guide. Finally, in the first volume of his *Studien zur Anthroposophie* ('Studies in Anthroposophy', Norderstedt, 2007, not translated), Michael Muschalle offers in-depth reflections about Rudolf Steiner's method of observing thinking, along with its various commentators.

Synthesis of percepts and concepts

In his book, *Philosophy of Freedom*, Rudolf Steiner summarizes his method of enquiry into the nature of knowledge:

> Perception...is not something finished, completed. It constitutes only one side of total reality. The other side is conceptual. The act of knowing is a synthesis between percepts and concepts. Only when the percept and the concept of a thing are united do they make that thing whole and complete.[30]

According to Steiner, by bringing together percepts and concepts in the act of knowing we create 'total reality'. Reality thus *emerges* from a process within our own cognitive mind.[31]

In *Philosophy of Freedom*, Rudolf Steiner elucidates his interpretation of knowledge from many points of view, ever deepening and broadening the overall idea of knowledge. For example, in the chapter entitled, 'The consequences of monism', he states in truly Aristotelian spirit:

> Perception is the part of reality that is given objectively, while concepts are a part that is given subjectively (through intuition). Our internal mental structure splits reality into these two components. One component appears as perceptions, the other as concepts. Only through the union of the two—i.e. through perceptions lawfully integrated into the cosmos—do we find the fullness of reality. If we consider percepts in isolation we don't get reality but only disjointedness and chaos. If we limit ourselves to searching for lawful connections between percepts, all we end up with is abstract concepts. Abstract concepts do not possess any reality— but thoughtful observation does when we see percepts and concepts not in isolation but in their correlations.[32]

Thus, Steiner sees in the cognitive process a conscious attempt to make whole and complete a reality which we experience as split apart into our perceptions and concepts. One could object that percepts are hardly an objective given. Indeed, perception may be regarded as a purely subjective experience within human consciousness. However, Steiner's understanding of 'subjective' and 'objective' in this context is not at all the same as the standard one. Ordinarily, the term *subjective* is regarded as synonymous with 'personal', 'relative', 'not provable'. The antonym *objective* is taken to mean ' factual' or 'generally valid'. For Steiner, however, the word *objective* means simply 'stemming from an object', and *subjective*, 'springing from a subject'. That is to say: Steiner calls *objective* anything that comes to meet us from the outside, from the objects themselves, while calling *subjective* anything that is generated within us. According to these definitions, then, a *tree* will be an objective percept, while a *feeling* is a subjective one.

Steiner places thinking *above and beyond* both subjective and objective because it is thinking that allows us to distinguish these two categories in the first place. Thinking is *neither* subjective *nor* objective but antecedes both categories—as indeed it does all other concepts. In positive terms: thinking is *universal*.

In a significant footnote to his *Grundlinien einer Erkenntnistheorie der Goetheschen Weltanschauung* ('Outline of a theory of Knowledge of Goethe's Worldview'), Rudolf Steiner elaborates further on his theory of knowledge:

> Thus the question, What is knowledge? has been answered in principle. The answer will not change if we widen the question to include spirit vision. That is why what I have said in this book about the essence of knowledge relates equally to knowledge of the spiritual worlds, as I have described it in my later writings. The sensory world does not present itself to human perception as full reality. It becomes reality only in combination with what thinking reveals about it. Thoughts belong of necessity to the reality of what is perceived through the senses. It is just that the thought component of what we perceive with our senses does not reach us from the outside—along with our sense perceptions—but rather from the inside, from within the human being. Yet in reality thought and sensory perception are of *one and the same* essence. By meeting the world through the medium of our sensory

perceptions, we humans separate off thought from reality; but the thought only re-appears in a different place, inside the soul. The separation of percept and concept has no significance whatever for the objective universe. It only occurs because humans insert themselves existentially into the world. Consequently, the impression is created—for *us* only—as if thought and sense perception were two completely different realities. It is no different in the case of spiritual vision. When spirit vision arises by means of the soul processes I have described in my later book, *Wie erlangt man Erkenntnisse der höheren Welten?* ['How to Know Higher Worlds'], it too forms only one side of spiritual existence; the other side is the corresponding thoughts about the spiritual world. The only difference is that, in a certain way, we experience the full reality of *sensory perception* as being completed in an *upward direction,* towards the beginnings of the spiritual—while the true essence of *spiritual vision* is experienced as descending from its starting point in a *downward direction*. It makes no difference *in principle* that sensory experiences take place by means of sense organs created by nature, while spirit vision requires spiritual organs that first have to be developed in the soul.[33]

We see here how truly comprehensive Steiner's concept of knowledge is, with distinct characteristics in different areas of application. In the natural sciences, for instance, enquiry is directed chiefly toward the organic and inorganic realms. In philosophy, the focus is on human thinking and actions. Going beyond these, anthroposophical spiritual science[34] aims for knowledge of the supersensible (metaphysical) realities of the universe. Yet in each case we are dealing with the same basic dynamics: questions arise from something we have perceived [German: *ein Wahrnehmbares*] and are answered by forming the corresponding thoughts [German: *Gedankenbildungen*].

Our argument is beginning to move from philosophy towards anthroposophical spiritual science. Methodologically, we are still aiming to define the category of knowledge with precision and to take hold vigorously of the being that makes this category real—the I. In fact, the category of knowledge, defined as the combination between the perceptions that are given and the concepts we create, can be seen as the *core category* of the human I. For only the human I can turn knowledge into a *lived reality*. We might go so far as to say that the human I, being 'located' within a physical body and holding the centre of the life of the soul, is itself *the cause of the split* in our noetic world. For it is only the peculiar structure of our human organism that divides the world into what we perceive and what we think. Things *in themselves* exist in an undivided unity of perception and concept, of appearance and cosmic lawfulness.

To make this clearer let us return to the example of the beech tree from before. Whatever we know about the laws that regulate the growth of beeches is a real, operative principle *in nature*, while *in our consciousness* this principle manifests as something purely ideal and abstract, utterly devoid of life and power. We may speak of *real events* versus *ideal events*. *Real events* are actual processes or events in the universe or in nature that may become the objects of perception (and thereafter of reflection as well). By contrast, *ideal events* only take place on the level of consciousness in the forming of concepts, the objects of thinking. One might say: The cognitive process combines *real events* (i.e. forces) in the form of *perceptions* with *ideal events* (i.e. laws) in the form of *concepts*. Thus the wholeness of reality is restored.

Johann Gottlieb Fichte and the discovery of the I

Having explored the idea of knowledge, we can now take a fresh look at self-conscious being and I-consciousness. In this context it is rewarding to turn our attention to Johann Gottlieb Fichte (1762-1814), a thinker whose entire striving established him as the philosopher of the I par excellence. Throughout the numerous versions and revisions of his theory of science, Fichte keeps reaching for an ever deeper understanding of the I. In trying to establish the theoretical underpinnings of his theory Fichte's searches for a single unconditional principle underlying all human knowledge. He finds it in the statement 'A is A', or 'A equals A'. Prompted by this statement, self-evident in itself, Fichte observes that our mind clearly has the power to posit *something*—anything, regardless of what exactly that thing may be; thus: A. We simply posit by an act of thinking, 'When A is true, then A is true'. Therefore, what is posited absolutely by the thinking mind is the *form* rather than the specific *content* of the statement.

This is the basis on which Fichte now approaches the I. The form of the logically evident statement 'A equals A' is designated as X and is understood by Fichte to be posited by the thinking I.

> X, at least, must be *in* the I, and posited *by* the I. For in the statement above it is the I that judges with reference to X as its law, which therefore must be a given for the I. And because it is posited absolutely and not derived from anything else, it must follow that the I is given X by the I itself.[35]

According to Fichte, the capacity of the I to posit something in itself and through itself is grounded in the phrase, 'I am I'.

> The statement, 'I am I' is valid absolutely and unconditionally, for it is the same as statement X. It is true not only in its form but also in its content. In it, the I is posited not conditionally but absolutely, under the predicate of identity with itself; it is therefore posited [German: *gesetzt*]; and the statement [German: *Satz*] can also by expressed in this way: *I am*.

Fichte is saying that when the I thinks itself as 'I am I', it actually *posits* itself in a *Tathandlung* ['act/action'] of the spirit.[36] That is to say, the form of thinking gives itself its own content—the I— through the I itself.

> The positing of the I through itself is purely its own activity.—The I posits *itself* and it *is* merely by the power of its own act of positing. Conversely, the I *is* and *posits* its being merely by the power of its own being. It is at one and the same time actor and product of its action; the activity and that which is produced by that activity.

> Act and action are coinciding. Hence the *I am* is the expression of
> a *Tathandlung* ['act/action'].

In this sequence of arguments we can experience how the thinking I grasps itself. Fichte belabours this point page after page
in quasi-meditative thought circles. Again and again he tries to
bring to expression the self-positing of the I, the prime and absolute *Tathandlung* of the spirit.

> The I is that entity whose being [German: *Sein*] or substance
> [German: *Wesen*] consists only in positing itself as being, as an
> absolute subject. It is such as it posits itself. Therefore the I is
> absolute and necessary for the I. Anything that is not itself is not
> an I. ... The I *is* only insofar as it is conscious of itself.

With the last sentence of the quote above we have reached a
critical point in Fichte's philosophy. Fichte could have taken his
understanding of the I as a *starting point*—an adequate meta-
phor since the I can hardly be considered more than a point—for
exploring the I's real potential for seeing into the realm of the
supersensible. Instead, Fichte oversteps the mark and veers off
into sheer speculation. Generalizing from the idea that the I *does
not truly exists* without awareness of itself—an assertation that is
just about defensible—Fichte performs a fatal backflip of logical
deduction when he pronounces:

> All that is is only insofar as it is posited within the I. There is
> nothing outside the I.

For Fichte, then, the I is the only category of reality. Clearly,
Fichte made an enormous contribution by searching for the
I—but having found it he misinterpreted it seriously. His
interpretation makes him lose sight of the reality of the world.
After his logical somersault there is no other place for Fichte
to go than to return to the point of the self-positing I over
and over again, as if mesmerized by it. There simply isn't any
meaningful content that follows from Fichte's solipsistic interpretation of the I.

Avoiding Fichte's mistake we move on to consider Rudolf Steiner's concept of knowledge. Steiner makes the critical point that by knowing itself the I does not only realize *itself*. It is also capable of *realizing the category of knowledge in the broadest way*. In this way, the I can encompass *the whole world as the contents of its cognitive activity*.

Linking up with our previous discussion on the concept of substance, we can now characterize the two poles of self-knowledge more precisely than Fichte did. Self-knowledge is established by the cognitive effort of each individual human being. Each person's thinking impulse (or thinking activity) constitutes *reality* in the sense of Aristotle's *first substances*—the reality in which single individuals are present. The ideal content grasped by the thinking activity of the conscious I are the essence of the I, in the Platonic sense.

But there is more: in the process of self-knowledge a fusion occurs between Aristotelian real events and Platonic ideal events. Self-knowledge as a whole must comprise both. It makes no sense to consider the fusion between real events and ideal events *in isolation*, outside of the I's knowledge of itself. On the contrary, only in actual, real-time self-knowledge does this fusion truly happen. The principles and forces that are operative in the laws of nature, quite independently of human consciousness, are experienceable in our self-knowledge only to the extent that our self-knowledge itself is an immediately experienceable real event (i.e. the will to think). The experience of self-knowledge, then, is linked in a feedback loop with the various thought contents that correspond to the forces of nature. It follows that the primal unity of nature is recreated with respect to the human I by means of its experience of itself.

The coincidence and fusion of real events and ideal events in the I's knowledge of itself means nothing less than the *reconciliation of Platonism and Aristotelianism*. At the same time, it marks the *birth of anthroposophical spiritual science*.

We have reached the limit of what can be communicated by the written word. The process we are describing can be pressed into definitions but in such definitions the primal, living, creative self-knowledge of the I dies away. An example of such a 'dead' definition of the I might run as follows: *The I is a being that actualizes knowing and realizes itself in the process of knowing. Knowing is a category of the I.*

This definition offers a very concentrated abstract of what we have tried to introduce as *lived experience* in exploring the self-knowledge of the I.

Taking our cue from Fichte, our aim in this section was to nudge readers towards actualizing their own I-awareness as a concrete, individual noetic process. At the same time, we have tried to characterize three different positions on the question of substance from the history of philosophy: Platonism, Aristotelianism, and their union in Rudolf Steiner's theory of science.

What all this means for the seeker of knowledge

What have we learned in this chapter that can be of benefit to the individual seeker of knowledge? Observing our own cognitive process has helped us formulate a theory of knowledge that can serve as a dependable framework for our own questions. Living noetic practice means taking human individuality into account. That is to say, the *different ways* in which we elaborate and combine percepts and concepts in the cognitive process are an important part of own core identity. The most immediate result of our cognitive activities is the production of *mental images*—the various images of what we have first grasped in our mind, later recalled with the help of memory. Our capacity to *remember* mental images suggests that these products of our cognitive process remain connected with our essential being. They can therefore be viewed as *subjective projections* of the total reality we actualize during cognition ('subjective' in the sense 'appearing in the subject', as discussed previously). This is why in *Philosophy of Freedom* Rudolf Steiner refers to such mental images as 'individualized concepts'.

The sum total of our mental images is the treasure house of our personal experiences. Mental images will be all the richer the more we are able to experience the world through our senses *as well as* our minds. There are at least two ways we individualize concepts when making mental images: first, through the great variety of sensory contents that each concept is connected to; and secondly, by the many ways in which concepts relate to us as individuals. The latter is individualized even further since we not only *know* things but also have *feelings* about them. Rudolf Steiner regards this as crucially important for human individuality. In the *Philosophy of Freedom* he states:

> Our thinking connects us with the world; but it is our feelings that lead us back to ourselves. Only thus are we made into true individuals. ... If we only had *knowledge* of ourselves we would remain utterly indifferent to ourselves—but in addition to our self-knowledge we are also possessed of 'self-feeling'. Feelings of pleasure or pain accompany our various perceptions. Only thus are we able to live as individuals whose existence is not reduced to their cognitive relationship with the surrounding world but who attach a definite value to the world and to themselves.[37]

Let us weigh the import of these words properly. They suggest that we humans can only find ourselves by means of our feelings. Without feelings our self-knowledge would be pointless. Our motivation in seeking to know ourselves is itself *a matter of feeling*. This fact must never be overlooked or underestimated. It is an essential ingredient among the real events of self-knowledge. Fichte put all his emphasis on a purely conceptual understanding of the I. He completely overlooked the real *emotional need* to know ourselves, which underlies and drives our will to think. Ultimately, this is the reason Fichte's approach is sterile when it comes to understanding the reality of human experience.

Rudolf Steiner goes even further and warns of the dangers of a one-sided kind of thinking that leads to pure abstraction:

> The further we move upwards in the direction of a universalized thinking where the individual is considered no longer of any interest except as a specimen or to illustrate a concept, the more the character of uniqueness, the quality of being a particular, single personality, will get lost in us.[38]

With all due respect for the central role of thinking in the noetic process, it has to be admitted that thinking can also 'dry up' our humanness unless we cultivate a healthy capacity for distancing ourselves from our thinking and thus protect and preserve our feelings and perceptions.

Yet Steiner also points out the opposite danger. We can lose ourselves in feelings that are too one-sided and egocentric. Ideally, our individuality arises from a harmonious, rhythmical movement—rather like the swinging of a pendulum—between thinking, perceiving and feeling. Let us aspire to 'take along' our feelings to wherever we go with our minds. Then our knowledge will still take on a human countenance.

In the next part of our journey we examine the fusion between Platonic and Aristotelian thought in the development of spiritual science. We will ask how knowledge becomes humanized—which will lead us to the heart of *anthroposophy*. But first we will turn once again to the words of Plato and Aristotle. There are methodological reasons for doing so. Indeed, our interest in realms of spirit beings is awakened at the very moment when our self-knowledge also begins to dawn. It is important ever and again to immerse ourselves in the historic and spiritual foundations that have carried us up to the point where the I appears. A deeper understanding of our own foundations helps build the inner resources we need for knowing and meeting spiritual beings in a safe and wholesome way.

9. Platonism, Aristotelianism and the knowledge of spiritual beings

Before proceeding as suggested we need to take a closer look at the field of tension between Platonism and Aristotelianism. Our aim is not to write a history of philosophy or to present a meta-scientific analysis. The problems of Platonism vs Aristotelianism are only relevant for us insofar as they show how deeply Platonic and Aristotelian worldviews are rooted *in the human soul* where they compete with each other and complement each other in hidden, metamorphosed ways.

Plato's philosophy divides the world sharply between appearances and ideas, between becoming and being, and on the epistemological level, between opinion and knowledge. His dialogues develop the idea of a dual partition of reality from many aspects. In the *Timaios*, a late work concerning the creation of the cosmos, Plato's theory finds its quintessential expression:

> First then, in my judgment, we must make a distinction and ask, What is that which always is and has no becoming, and what is that which is always becoming and never is? That which is apprehended by intelligence and reason is always in the same state, but that which is conceived by opinion with the help of sensation and without reason is always in a process of becoming and perishing and never really is. [39]

It is characteristic of Plato's thinking that he merges knowledge with moral virtue. Knowledge is presented as inseparable from truth but also from absolute goodness and beauty.

> Let me tell you then why the creator made this world in generation. He was good... [40]
>
> The work of the creator, whenever he looks to the unchangeable and fashions the form and nature of his work after an unchangeable pattern, must necessarily be made fair and perfect, but when he looks to the created only and uses a created pattern, it is not fair and perfect. [41]

The latter quote highlights some of the problems with Plato's philosophy. As the world of both ideas and appearances is judged from a moral point of view ('a created pattern…is not fair and perfect'), the whole system gets somehow caught in a cleft stick. The sense-perceptible world is in danger of being reduced to a *mere image* while the world of ideas or 'forms' is given an *archetypal character*. Individual things are nothing but more or less perfect imitations (by *mimesis*) of their corresponding eternal, archetypal ideas. This is expressed in the Platonic concept of *participation* (*methexis*), according to which each individual object participates in the universal being of its corresponding idea.

Platonism has had a lasting influence on the development of philosophy. Even today it is considered one of the cornerstones of Western thought. Rudolf Steiner, though himself a stern critic of Platonism including its later Christian versions, nonetheless expressed his respect:

> It is fair to say that the philosophy of Plato is the most lofty system of thought ever to have issued forth from the human spirit. Platonism embodies the conviction that the ultimate goal of knowledge is to reach the *ideas* that sustain the world and are its foundation.[42]

If we allow Plato's philosophy to affect us on an experiential level we discover that it has a strong upward movement with the power to lift, develop, purify and spiritualize the soul. However, this upward thrust becomes problematic when it is combined with a tendency to turn away from the world of the senses. It is true that even a rather one-sided, other-worldly version of Platonism still has something of spiritual value to offer to humanity—but only at the expense of the riches of experience and knowledge that belong to the physical world.

The philosophy of Aristotle pursues a very different goal. Aristotle aims at seeing concepts and ideas *within* the objects, rather than *separated* from their sensory appearance. This emerges most clearly from Aristotle's teaching in one of his most famous treatises, entitled *Categories*. Here Aristotle lists ten categories and develops them as conceptual tools for a highly differentiated understanding of the world. He starts off in his trademark method, in a very grounded, hands-on manner. With a number of simple examples from the sense world he gradually moves his argument to an absolute pinnacle of intellectual abstraction—yet without ever losing the connection with sensory reality.

In the opening of the fourth chapter, Aristotle introduces all ten categories at once:

> Of things said without any combination, each signifies either *substance* or *quantity* or *qualification* or a *relative* or *where* or *when* or *being-in-position* or *having* or *doing* or *being-affected*. To give a rough idea, examples of *substance* are man, horse; of *quantity*: four-foot, five-foot; of *qualification*: white, grammatical; of a *relative*: double, half, larger; of *where*: in the Lyceum, in the market place; of *when*: yesterday, last year; of *being-in-a-position*: is-lying, is-sitting; of *having*: has-shoes-on, has-armour-on; of *doing*: cutting, burning; of *being-affected*: being cut, being-burned.[43]

Taken together, the ten categories form a structured spiritual organism which we can summarize as follows:

Substance—The essence or substrate.
Answers the question: Who or what?

Quantity—The number and measure of substances.
Answers the question: How much?

Quality—The consistency and attributes of substances.
Answers the question: How?

Relation—The mutual connections between substances.
Answers the question: What correlations?

Space—The location of substances in relation to each other.
Answers the question: Where?

Time—The sequence of substances following one another. Answers the question: When?

Position—The status of substances. Answers the question: In what position?

Having—The manner of being of substances. Answers the question: What does the substance possess?

Doing—The activity of substances. Answers the question: What does the substance do?

Being-affected—The passivity of substances. Answers the question: What does the substance receive?

The hierarchic arrangement of the Aristotelian categories is very noticeable. In the first position we find the category of substance or essence. Indeed, substance 'underlies' all the rest, for quantity, quality, relation, and the rest are all predicated about a substance, about a 'something'. We could say with Aristotle that all the other categories *manifest* or are occasioned by the first category which is *substance*. The stepped structure of the system leads on from the larger categories to the smaller ones, from the more general to the more particular. *Quantity* and *quality*, for example, are permanently linked with the nature of being, while *doing* and *being-affected* both represent transient states of constant change. Thus the fact that a human being—a 'two-footed living being' according to Aristotle's definition in the *Metaphysics*—can be both a single individual (*quantity*) and artistically gifted (*quality*) is far more *essential* (i.e. closer to his or her essence) than the contingent realities of being at market (*location*) or listening to a concert (*being-affected*).

Characteristically, Aristotle's understanding of substance is at one and the same time both general and specific, abstract and concrete. Aristotle avoids creating an unpassable gap between concrete things and abstract ideas. His understanding of substances takes in both *materiality* and *spiritual form*:

> We call substances (1) the simple bodies , i.e. earth and fire and water and everything of the sort, and in general bodies and the things composed of them, both animals and divine beings, and the parts of these ... (2) That which, being present in such things as are not predicated of a subject, is the cause of their being, as soul is the being of animals. ... It follows, then, that substance has two senses, (a) the ultimate substratum, which is no longer predicated of anything else, and (b) that which is a 'this' and separable—and of this nature is the shape or form of each thing.[44]

In one sense, then, *substance* means the *cause of being*, the underlying form, the 'ultimate substratum which is no longer predicated of anything else'. Here Aristotle is looking *from above*, as it were. At the same time, substance also indicates something concrete, compounded of matter and form, such as the living beings on the earth and the celestial bodies in the heavens. That is the empirical aspect, the Aristotelian perspective *from below*.

Just like Plato's ideas, Aristotle's philosophy casts a long shadow over the two subsequent millennia. His teachings on logic were at all times recognized as masterpieces of dialectic analysis. Nonetheless, we may ask ourselves whether Aristotelian thought, and especially Aristotle's understanding of substance, was in fact ever properly received and understood. When Rudolf Steiner examined the historic influence of Platonism and Aristotelianism in his book, *Goethe's Worldview*, he answered in the negative:

> In vain did Aristotle rebel against Plato's dualistic view of the world. He saw nature as a unified being that contains ideas just as much as it contains sensory objects and phenomena. Only in the human mind do ideas have independent existence. But this independence does not imply that ideas possess their own separate

reality. It is the soul alone that separates out ideas from sensory objects which together constitute reality.[45]

Assessing the effect of Aristotelianism on the soul, we notice that Aristotelian thinking generates a mood of *keen interest and curiosity* about everything we encounter in the world, whether of a physical, soul or spiritual nature. Aristotelianism makes us turn outward, towards the world and towards the earth. This outlook can become problematic in turn when a one-sided focus on physical matter causes us to disconnect from the spiritual foundations of the world. This disconnect has happened in the natural sciences of the modern period and goes against the true spirit of Aristotelian philosophy.

Thomas Aquinas and the science of angels

Following the threads of Platonic and Aristotelian influences throughout history we encounter the figure of Thomas Aquinas (1225-1274), a thinker in whom the two streams merged quite congenially, especially in relation to the knowledge of spiritual beings. Thomas' unfinished treatise, *On the nature of angelic beings* (*'De substantiis separatis seu de angelorum natura'*) is dedicated to his friend and collaborator, Reginald of Piperno. In this book, Aquinas follows the scholastic method in comparing and contrasting various statements about spiritual beings made by Plato and Aristotle, evaluating them point by point, clarifying what they have in common and where they differ. It is truly rewarding to look at Plato and Aristotle through the lens of this outstanding medieval mind. Here is what Thomas Aquinas has to say about Plato:

> Plato posited certain natures, separate from the matter of flowing things, in which truth [*veritas*—reality *SH*] remained abiding. By adhering to these natures, our soul knew the truth [reality *SH*]. Hence, as the mind (*intellectus*) in knowing truth apprehends certain things beyond the matter of sensible things, Plato thus believed that there existed certain truths [realities *SH*] separate from sensible things.[46]

Aquinas goes on to describe what Plato says about the two kinds of abstraction by which the mind grasps the truth as separate from matter, namely *mathematical concepts* and *universal ideas*:

> Now our intellect uses a two-fold abstraction in arriving at the understanding of truth: One, according as it grasps mathematical numbers, magnitudes, and figures without the understanding of sensible matter; for, in understanding the number two or three, or a line, a surface, a triangle, or a square, there is not included together with it in our apprehension anything pertaining to what is hot or cold, or the like, which is perceptible by sense. Our mind (*intellectus*), however, uses another abstraction when it understands something universal without the consideration of something particular, as when we understand a human being without including in our understanding anything about Socrates, Plato, or any other individual.[47]

This forms the backdrop for the hierarchic structure of being in Plato's worldview which Aquinas summarizes as follows:

> In this way, therefore, between us and the highest God, it is clear that [the Platonists] posited four orders, namely, that of the secondary gods, that of the separate intellects, that of the heavenly souls, and that of the good or wicked demons. If all these things were true, then all these intermediate orders would be called by us 'angels'.[48]

Thomas' critique of Plato is particularly interesting, as it reveals the fundamentally Aristotelian orientation of his scholastic mind:

> But the basis of this position is found to be without foundation, for it is not necessary that what the intellect understands separately [from matter *SH*] should have a separate existence [from matter *SH*] in reality. Hence, neither should we posit separate universals (*universalia*) subsisting (*subsistentia*) outside singulars nor likewise mathematicals outside sensible things; for universals are

the essences (*essentiae*) of particular things themselves and mathematicals are certain limits (*terminationes*) of sensible bodies.[49]

In this last statement, Plato's dualist split of reality is roundly rejected. In the next part of his argument, Thomas turns to Aristotle and his understanding of spiritual entities. First he refers to the Aristotelian concept of the 'unmoved mover' from the *Metaphysics*. Aquinas writes:

> First, (Aristotle) established by both reason and examples, the fact that everything moved is moved by another; and that if something is said to be self-moved, this is not true of it according to the same part but according to diverse parts of itself, so that one part is moving and another is moved. Furthermore, since we are not to proceed into infinity with movers and things moved, because if the first mover is taken away, it would follow that the other movers as well would not be moved, we must therefore arrive at some first unmoved mover and some first movable which is moved by itself, in the manner already indicated; for that which is through itself, is prior to and the cause of that which is through another.[50]

Here we encounter the idea of a first mover who sets all things in motion without being himself moved by anything (or rather: who receives his self-movement only from himself). The idea of the 'unmoved mover' leads directly to the Aristotelian conception of God which casts the question about the nature of spiritual beings in an entirely new light, since spiritual beings are thought to dwell between God and humans.

The first unmoved mover must contain the goal ('whereto') and the reason ('why') of his movement within himself—otherwise he would in some way be moved from outside himself. Likewise, the first mover has to be thought of as beyond space and time. He is non-spatial because he moves with unlimited power—for if he did not move with unlimited power there would be other self-moving entities beside him and beyond him, and hence he would not be the *first* mover. But everything in space is limited by its location. On account of his unlimited power, therefore, the unmoved mover must be non-spatial. Likewise, the unmoved mover must be non-temporal because all movement in time begins with him. The development of all beings is grounded in his being which is therefore outside of time or, in a word, eternal.

Aristotle's concept of movement, taken together with his particular understanding of matter, leads to the idea that everything that is moved is of a *material* nature while the mover himself *is non-material*. It follows that the entire visible cosmos, in all its mobility and materiality, is moved by non-material, spiritual powers (movers). In the words of Thomas Aquinas:

> Therefore each of the heavenly bodies is animated by its own soul and each has its own separate desirable object which is the proper end of its motion. ... There are, accordingly, many separate substances that are in no way united to any bodies; there are, likewise, many intellectual substances united to heavenly bodies. Aristotle attempts to find out the number of these on the basis of the number of motions of the heavenly bodies.[51]

It is very characteristic of Aristotelian thinking to build an understanding of *spiritual* entities by starting from a *sensory* point of view—in this case from the celestial bodies, i.e. from astronomy. Aquinas, however, is not satisfied with this approach and wants to go further. He offers a most striking criticism of Aristotle:

> Now this position of Aristotle seems to be surer because it does not depart greatly from that which is evident according to sense; yet it seems to be less adequate than the position of Plato. In the first place, there are many things which are evident according to the senses, for which an explanation cannot be given on the basis of what Aristotle teaches. For we see in men who are possessed by devils and in the works of sorcerers, certain phenomena which do not seem capable of taking place except through some intellectual substance. ... Secondly, (Aristotle's position seems less adequate)

because it seems unbefitting that immaterial substances should be limited to the number of corporeal substances. For those beings that are higher do not exist for the sake of those that are lower. But on the contrary, that because of which something else exists, is the more noble.[52]

Thomas argues against Aristotle that it is impossible to determine the number of spiritual beings from the number of moving celestial bodies. To gain a comprehensive understanding of spiritual realities it is not enough to consider sensory realities alone.

The spiritual mission of Thomas Aquinas

Thomas Aquinas' impulse is of major significance in spiritual history. His writings constitute an attempt to unite the intellectual tradition of antiquity with the revelations of Holy Scripture. Aquinas seeks to discover as much agreement as possible between the two traditions, while keeping the border between Christian faith and the science of philosophy rather fluid. Grounded in the mental discipline of philosophy and intensely committed to Catholic orthodoxy, Thomas Aquinas lays out a highly complex and arcane vision of the angelic world. At the root of the Thomistic concept of angels lie statements such as the following:

> For those substances which share in 'to be' most perfectly, do not have in themselves something which is a being only in potency. That is why they are called immaterial substances.[53]

There are many levels of meaning here. The key is the idea of *sharing (or participating) in being.* Being in this context means the Being of the unmoved mover, God. Some entities are said to share in this Being in the most perfect way possible. If a being shares in the Being of God with the highest level of participation then nothing remains in that being that can be viewed as mere potential ('in potency'). For potential implies the possibility to evolve in one direction or another—but having the potential for change is incompatible with the idea of perfection, or reality. If a being is perfect then it is wholly *real* or *realized*, that is, it has the complete *actuality* of a perfected being. Maximum participation in the divine Being must therefore exclude potentiality. What is more, the philosophical tradition of Aristotle regards the concept of potentiality as equivalent to the concept of *matter*, just as *reality* corresponds to the concept of *form*. That is why Aquinas describes spiritual beings as *non-material*. We might also call them *beings of pure form*.

There is a question that was hotly debated among the medieval scholastics: 'How can there be a plurality of spiritual beings, distinct from one another, if each consists of nothing but pure form?'

Behind this question is an assumption that beings differ only in regard to their *physical bodies*. Thomas Aquinas, quick to defend the significance of forms, makes a forceful argument against this assumption:

> Therefore among the higher substances to which the potency of matter is completely foreign, there is found a difference of greater or lesser refinement according to the difference in the perfection of the form; but there is in them no composition of matter and form.[54]

Thus, according to the Thomistic view, angels are not composed of matter and form. Instead, angels are *pure form*, complete reality. Nonetheless, Aquinas maintains the idea of a hierarchic order among the angels, based on the greater or lesser refinement of their form.

> Therefore in every being other than the first, there is present both a 'to be' itself as the act [*actus*, reality *SH*], and the substance having the 'to be' as a potency receptive of the act of 'to be'.[55]

The 'receptive potency' of a purely spiritual being—an angel—must be understood as part of its real being. Even so, the receptive potency of different spiritual beings may reflect different levels of development. To put it another way: unlike human bodies, the bodies of angels (their 'materiality') have the capacity to *receive the divine Being*. The receptive potency of angels, their 'corporeality', is indeed so pure and refined that divine reality can pour itself into it without intermediary, leaving not the slightest residue of potentiality, as would be the case with human bodies. The distance between humans and God is thus attributed to the spiritual 'coarseness' of our human corporeality which always retains a portion of mere potential, or matter. What exists undivided in the angels—potency and reality, matter and form—is split apart in us.

*

By way of conclusion, we would like to mention a fascinating controversy in Thomistic thought which turns on the question: 'Were the angels created by God or are they uncreated beings?' The contentious nature of the question is obvious from the following set of arguments. First, everything that comes into being must have a cause. This cause must lie outside of its own being. But 'becoming' only takes place within matter. Therefore, since angels are not material, it appears they cannot have come into being. Secondly, 'becoming' means either 'being moved' or 'being changed'. But since the medium of all movement is *matter* which exists only as potentiality it would seem that the angels, as non-material beings, cannot be moved, and therefore cannot have been created. Thirdly, angels are pure forms and their forms are eternal, but how could something eternal have been created?

These arguments strongly suggest that angels, being pure forms, do not originate in time and are not caused by anything outside of themselves. Therefore the angels would appear to be uncreated eternal beings, having their origin only in themselves. For Aquinas, this line of argument, however much rooted in Platonic and Aristotelian philosophy, creates a direct conflict with the Catholic belief that God created all beings. In the introduction of *On Separate Substances* Thomas makes it clear where his allegiance lies:

> [W]e shall be in a position to accept whatever we find that agrees
> with faith, and refute whatever is opposed to Catholic teaching.[56]

Hence Thomas feels compelled to reject as unorthodox the idea
that the angels are uncreated eternal beings:

> Furthermore, it is contrary to Christian teaching that spiritual
> substances should be said to derive their origin from the highest
> deity in such a way that they should have been from eternity—as
> the Platonists and the Peripatetics [i.e. Aristotelians *SH*] held. But,
> on the contrary, the declaration of the Catholic faith has it that
> they began to be after they had previously not existed.[57]

Maintaining the idea that God created all things as postulated
by faith—which of necessity includes the angels—causes Aquinas to perform a brilliant if rather dizzying feat of reasoning. It
would be unfair to accuse Thomas of simply forcing his thoughts
into the straightjacket of faith, come what may. We should rather
seek to understand how Aquinas managed to turn a rather existential dilemma into something positive and fruitful.

Thomas mounts his first attack by accusing the argument
against the angels' createdness of 'hidden materialism'. The
problem of creation and origins, he insists, is approached too
narrowly from the perspective of matter. Instead of looking at
the question 'from below', as it were, Aquinas instead proposes
to look at it 'from above', from the perspective of God:

> Therefore, above the mode of coming to be, by which some-
> thing becomes when form comes to matter, we must presuppose
> another origin for things according as 'to be' is bestowed upon the
> whole universe of things by the First Being that is its own 'to be'.[58]

On the premise that angels are both immaterial beings and created by God, Aquinas opens up the following line of argument:

> For every motion is *from* this determinate point *to* that determinate
> point, and every change is the terminus of some motion. There-
> fore, over and above the mode of becoming by which something

comes to be through change or motion, there must be a mode of becoming or origin of things, without any mutation or motion through the influx of being.[59]

From this perspective then, it can be said that the angels were not created by 'motion' (which would necessitate the presence of matter) but rather through an 'influx' of divine being. For this kind of movement to be carried out, no outside medium such as matter is required.

> [F]or according to this kind of making, for a subject to come to be is for the subject to participate in 'to be' through the influence [influx *SH*] of a higher being.[60]

The argument culminates in a rather paradoxical formulation:

> But in those things which come to be without change or motion through a simple emanation (*emanatio*) or influx (*influxus*), we are able to understand that something has been made without including that at some time, it did not exist. For when change or motion has been removed, there is not found in the action of the causal principle, the succession of 'before' and 'after'.[61]

From this is derived the qualified position that God creates the angels *continually* through a spiritual outpouring from above (beyond space and time)—which would still seem to imply that the angels have existed from eternity after all. But God's eternity is *more comprehensive* than that of the angels because angels receive their eternal being from God, not from themselves. To the human mind the angels thus appear simultaneously created and uncreated—a paradox that deftly achieves a reconciliation between philosophical reasoning and Christian doctrine.

When we allow the thought forms of Thomistic philosophy to act upon our souls we become aware of the subtle ways in which Aquinas navigates the field of tension between Platonism, Aristotelianism and Scripture. It is as if, by their very meeting in Aquinas' mind, each of these three different streams undergoes some kind of alchemical transformation. At the end of this process, Thomas Aquinas achieves a realistic view of the world of ideas that brings the angels within reach of our minds. In his writings we can experience 'angels on our mind' with great intensity. This begs the question whether Aquinas' scholastic approach to knowing angels can be adapted and developed further to fit the concerns and conditions of today.

10. Angelic encounters and spiritual-scientific investigation

The transition from medieval scholasticism to modern philosophy, especially towards German idealism, is marked by an awakening of self-consciousness and the individuality. Once full waking I-consciousness appears in spiritual evolution we must never lose it or let go of it. If we did we would open up a dangerous divide between ourselves and the conditions of our time. Our own development would be stunted. To keep in tune with conditions of our era we must take care to approach our relations with the angels from the perspective of the I.

In his essay, *Philosophy and Anthroposophy*, Rudolf Steiner describes a spiritual-scientific method of investigation that builds on a true understanding of I-consciousness:

> [The anthroposophical researcher *SH*] shuts off ordinary consciousness with the exception of the I, just as we experience it in pure thinking. The anthroposophical researcher then replaces their ordinary consciousness with a consciousness that is able to act comprehensively, in a way that parallels the way the I acts during pure thinking in ordinary consciousness.[62]

Metaphorically speaking, I-consciousness is a kind of point—an eye of the needle. Once we have passed through it, it begins to expand. It becomes a new periphery. This transformed I-periphery-consciousness is what anthroposophical spiritual science requires. How can we reach it in a way that is scientifically sound and meaningful? To rephrase according to the above quote, how *does* the I 'act during pure thinking in ordinary consciousness'?

In a previous chapter ('The concept of knowledge') we have seen how the thinker and the thought, ideal events and real events, coincide in the awareness of our own I. When we prepare for a noetic encounter with spiritual beings—beings from the angelic hierarchies—we similarly expect meaning and method to form a cognitive unity. In short, *what we know is determined by how we know it*.[63]

We are so used to our habitual, object-bound consciousness that we easily assume spiritual contents to be neatly separated from the methods we use to reach them. Not so in the cognitive method we are developing here! Things must never be taken in an abstract way. We are talking about a *living enactment* of cognition, a *journey* or *quest* in which we are deeply involved as seekers, with profound effects on our existence and the conduct of our lives.

While learning about the methods of cognition we also have learned about certain spiritual facts, such as the essential nature of thought and of the thinker. We know that for our ordinary consciousness, the I is the point where cognitive content and cognitive powers coincide. However, within the field of ordinary consciousness this 'I-point' is so singular and isolated from the rest of our experiences that it can be difficult for us to become fully aware of it. From the point of the *soul*, looking for the I is like searching about blindly in a thick cloud or fog. At the same time, this experience of blind searching actually conceals a high degree of *spiritual* clarity and purity which we should take as our inner standard as we prepare to step into the spiritual world.

Next we may ask ourselves: How can we conceive the essence of the angels above us—at least those who are closest to us? How can we, with fully awake I-consciousness, come to know the guardian spirit that accompanies each of us on our life's journey?

In looking for answers to such questions we can seek inspiration from the writings of John Scotus Eriugena, the ninth-century scholar whom we have already encountered in an earlier chapter:

> For, as we have said, he who has a pure understanding is created in that which he understands. So the intelligible and rational nature of the angel is created in the intelligible and rational nature of man just as the nature of man is created in the nature of angel, through the mutual knowledge by which an angel

understands man and man angel. There is nothing strange in this. For when we enter upon a discussion together the same thing happens: each of us is created in the other: for when I understand I am made your understanding, and in a certain way that cannot be described I am created in you. In the same way when you clearly understand what I clearly understand you are made my understanding, and of two understandings is made one, formed from that which we both clearly and without doubt understand. For example, to take an illustration from numerology, you understand that the number six is equal to its parts [i.e. the sum of its divisors *SH*]: and I understand the same thing, and understand that you understand it just as you understand that I understand. Each of our understandings, formed by the number six, has become one, and thus I am created in you and you are created in me. For we ourselves are not other than our understandings; for our true and ultimate essence is understanding specified by the contemplation of truth.[64]

The spiritual impulse expressed in these words is very much related to some of the historic figures we have encountered in previous chapters. For Eriugena, thinking is not merely the capacity to *reflect*. It can be experienced as an actual *creative force*. Thinking becomes creative when cognitive content and cognitive power are brought together and become one. When this happens in relation to angels, the human thinker becomes 'like the angels in heaven'. This leads to the notion of *interpenetration*. In a real inner encounter, different beings may interpenetrate each other without losing their own identity and integrity. Clearly, Eriugena does not in any way suggest that minds that know each other are dissolved when they meld and blend. Rather, we have to imagine—and work towards—a relation of mutual interpenetration that is very much like the relation between the essence of the I and the essence of thought during the act of cognition. In each case both sides preserve their identity.

In his book *Die Erwartung der Engel* ('Waiting for angels'), Wolf-Ulrich Klünker turns our attention to contemporary conditions and expands on the idea of 'noetic alignment' with the objects of our knowledge:

> Medieval theorists of knowledge worked out the notion of *adaequatio intellectus ad rem*, a kind of alignment or harmonizing of the human mind with its objects of knowledge. The effort of this alignment was experienced as a spiritual process that only related to thinking. Even in our own time it is still necessary to go through a process of harmonizing with the objects of knowledge. This is true especially in the case of spiritual matters, such as determining the hierarchic rank of an angel. But for us this *adaequatio* is no longer limited to purely mental activities. Instead, it affects the whole of human existence. We are, as it were, caught up in an existential process of spiritual harmonization which bestows on us the qualities of the Spirit Self. Of course, even medieval philosophers were convinced that by turning towards truth the whole human being would eventually be turned around and transformed. Yet the conditions that prevailed in the age of the intellectual soul prevented people from recognizing the full extent to which the *whole human body* is yearning for spiritual alignment—right down to the formation of the organs and of the blood.[65]

The effects of our striving for knowledge and of our orientation towards truth can indeed be felt all the way down into the various systems of the body. Sustained meditative practice can bring profound and remarkable changes in the way we relate to our body. For example, we may become much more aware how we 'sit' in our bodies differently during meditation. We experience how the centre of our mental concentration (the 'third eye', normally situated behind the forehead above the root of the nose) begins to shift its position, affecting our regular sense of life and our proprioception. Such sensations may occur quite spontaneously, including in the time between meditation sessions, and sometimes they can be downright unpleasant or irritating. For example, when our centre of concentration seems to shift *outside* our physical head we may feel literally 'beside ourselves'! These sorts of experiences demonstrate that there is a vital link between our inner practice and the very structure of our body, between consciousness [German: *Bewusstsein*] and existence [German: *Sein*]. They also show us that when we are existentially involved our noetic efforts are acting precisely on that link. How far we can go in observing the effects and resonances of our meditation, even down to our organs and cardiovascular system, will of course depend on our individual capacities.[66]

In the next chapter we shall look more closely at inner encounters with angels while further exploring Eriugena's idea about human beings becoming 'like unto the angels'.

11. Our guardian angels

Human destiny can be defined as the sum total of what a person manifests throughout their life. The concept of 'manifestation' offers a positive alternative to viewing life on earth as a mere conglomeration of more or less haphazard occurrences. After all, there must be a *being* that manifests. Human destinies can be seen as individual configurations bearing each person's unique *destiny signature*.

In considering questions of destiny we come once more upon certain limits, marked off by illness, sleep and death. These realities seriously challenge the conscious threads of our lives. Our waking consciousness is interrupted daily by the need for sleep. On a larger scale, all life ineluctably ends in death. How can we be sure that our destiny signature remains coherent and keeps its continuity when sickness, sleep and death make it impossible for us to grasp our destiny fully, let alone to shape it in complete consciousness?

Having asked these questions, we move to the idea of a *guardian angel*, imagined as a spirit associated with an individual human destiny, whose task is to preserve the integrity and continuity of our existence for as long as we are not able to do so ourselves.

Doubts about this way of thinking about guardian angels could be raised on two counts. First, it may be objected that we are indulging in mere fictions, chimeras without any grounding in reality. Secondly, we may demand certainty about the existence of angels through direct supersensible experience—an angelic manifestation.

Let us address these doubts by following our established methodology. We know that even our own I-being does not simply appear out of thin air but must first be *conceived* in thought. On this basis, it is easy to infer that other spiritual beings— including far more powerful ones than ourselves—may not appear to us without first being grasped in thought. It is true that the thought of the I is not the same as its reality; but only the thought of the I, when engaged with existentially, can lead to an actual experience of the reality of the I. The same holds true for angels. Granted, the idea of an angel is not its reality; but only by means of forming a *concept* of angels can we hope to come through to the *reality* of angels—at any rate, if we are committed to operating from the perspective of the I.

The German poet, Rainer Maria Rilke (1875-1926) summed up the challenge of angelic appearances in the phrase, 'Each angel is a burning terror'. In his *Duino Elegies*, Rilke powerfully describes the considerable limits placed on human encounters with angels:

> Who, if I cried, would hear me, of the angelic
> orders? or even supposing that one should suddenly
> carry me to his heart—I should perish under the pressure
> of his stronger nature. For beauty is only a step
> removed from a burning terror we barely sustain,
> and we worship it for the graceful sublimity
> with which it disdains to consume us. Each angel burns.[67]

The problem we encounter when experiencing angels is one of intensity, of *power*. Unprepared, we cannot bear the sight of angels. Power is much less of an issue when we *think* because thoughts move in a power-free zone of pure conceptualizations. Yet *pure thinking* has some powerful effects of its own. Over time it gives strength to our whole being. It helps us build up our 'spiritual spine', as it were. And it makes us fit for entering the powerful realm of the angels. When pure thinking is strengthened by meditation it is raised to an even higher level and can begin to play an active role in our destinies. In this way pure thinking changes into *living thinking*, into an organ that makes us ready for the experience of angels.

We may picture this process as a kind of 'double figure'. On one side of this figure, we reflect on events of our past. We discover patterns of destiny that had escaped us before. We remember perhaps how, at a certain time, we had to face some rather unpleasant life event, an event we wished we could have avoided and which pushed us in a direction we did not like. The event was followed by a long period of suffering. Our suffering was especially hard to bear because we could not make sense of what had happened to us—even though we tried. From a distance of several years, however, we *may* be able to see our past sufferings in a different light. We may reflect as follows: 'While I was dealing with my past sufferings I developed new capacities within me—capacities which are very useful to me now because they are supporting me in my new phase of life.' When we look back in this way and the patterns of destiny become clearer to us, it can even happen that a certain feeling of gratitude rises up in our soul—gratitude towards events we could only describe as terrifying and painful before.

This way of looking at life holds an important insight for us: *only the future reveals the true meaning of the past.* Yet interpreting the past is always a matter of individual choice. For we are free to think about our life and reflect on our past or not. Even so, whether consciously or unconsciously, the past will always appear in the light we ourselves bring to it. Shining forth this inner light is a gesture that helps to make thinking an integral, creative part of our destiny. We might call this activity *destiny imagination*. By this we mean a particular kind of conceptualization that helps us find the hidden links between the various threads that make the pattern of our destiny.

The practice of destiny imagination reaches deep into our feelings. It can influence our whole attitude towards life. We may rightly call it an *angelic perspective*. For it is our guardian angel who gives shape to the threads of our destiny and who knows the hidden destiny signature of our true being. When we begin to awaken to destiny imaginations, we are entering the sphere of the angels. Only, the angels have a different relationship to time than we do. Things that appear in sequence to us (for example when we look back at our past from some later vantage point) are experienced by the angels as *simultaneous*. It is as though the angels were looking down from above, along the axis of our lives, beholding everything in one grand display or tableau. This is because the angels do not experience reality and knowledge as separate.

The second part of the 'double figure' of living thinking is related to the first. Here we become aware that our meditative efforts can change the way we meet the present. Not only do we begin to perceive *more* but the *quality* of our perceptions changes. This experience can be somewhat startling, for we are so used to focus principally on understanding *meanings* intellectually. The shift in the quality of our perception caused by our meditative practice is an unexpected resonance from a hitherto undreamt-of realm—a good reason to take it seriously! To sum up: *our meditative efforts make the present, the future, and even the experiences of our own body, appear in a new light.*

In describing the 'double figure' of living thinking—sustained meditative reflection and its effects in real life—we have outlined a pathway by which we humans develop to become angel-like, growing gently into the sphere of our own guardian angel. It goes without saying that, like ordinary thinking, living thinking has to stand up to scrutiny with respect to its truth or untruth. When it comes to probing the truth of spiritual experiences, there is one critically important criterion. When a destiny imagination occurs as a result of concentrated meditative effort—and especially when an inspiration contains any directions or predictions about the future—the question to ask is: *Do I feel that I can follow this particular spiritual experience wholeheartedly in my mind and in my actions—or not?*

The truth or untruth of imaginations and inspirations can never be decided in a single moment but only over an extended period of time. Every true spiritual insight has a moral dimension. Destiny imaginations and the inspirations that arise from them present us with certain tasks. These tasks need to be honoured. For this reason the validity of spiritual insights cannot be decided by conceptual criteria alone. Our judgement must be based on what we have described as a *path of knowing*. On this path it is essential to *keep faith* with what we have once recognized as true. Walking the path of knowing involves listening and waiting patiently for what comes to meet us in due course by virtue of our faithfulness and our actions.

12. Angels don't lie

Do you not know that we are to judge angels?

1 Cor. 6:3

Human beings are caught in a constant push and pull between inner and outer experiences. From the outside the objects and processes of the world meet us through our perceptions. On the inside we experience our anxieties and sorrows, our joys and our hopes. In addition, thanks to our mind and our thinking, we can have insights of a logical or moral nature. And we are able to judge the truth or untruth of such insights without reliance on or reference to either external or internal phenomena.

Another remarkable feature of our human condition, both conscious and unconscious, is our ability to set our inner and outer worlds—our thoughts and our perceptions—in opposition to each other. We can point to a table and declare: 'This is a candlestick.' We can utter nonsense. We can tell lies.

When we lie we force our inner and outer experiences to diverge, to contradict each other—seemingly without any immediate adverse consequences. Sometimes we naively accept a whole range of false beliefs and it may take years before reality finally gets through and straightens us out.

It appears that human nature has the capacity to either grasp the truth out of its own resources or, on the contrary, to get mired in untruths and lies. Speaking generally, however, we may say that having a definite choice regarding our relationship to truth is a fundamental condition for human freedom.[68]

Errors and lies arise when, by the agency of some being, a *real process* (perception) and its corresponding *ideal process* (concept)—i.e. an external event and the concepts that makes it comprehensible—are separated from each other and then, by the same agency, put back together in a manner that contradicts factual reality. Hence, the precondition for errors and lies is a split between real processes and ideal processes in a being's consciousness. For humans, this split or gap exists almost anywhere in our relation to the world. Indeed, this is the very circumstance that urges us on to seek knowledge in the first place. The process of cognition is about reuniting the parts that have been split off from one another, our percepts and our concepts of the world. There is only one thing that is never divided, and that is the knowledge of our I, our own essential being. When we become aware of our own I-being we are lifted above and beyond the chasm that runs through our experience of the world, the gap that exists between our outside and inside experiences.[69]

Of course, the *real process* of I-consciousness depends very much on each person's individual efforts, based on their particular capacities and inclinations in any given place and time. Even so, with I-awareness the real process and the ideal process are not separated from each other. I-consciousness belongs to a category of universal conceptuality that determines its own content. Its content is simply the awareness that our own I is a cognitive being. The content of this awareness (i.e. our own being which recognizes itself as a self) does not exist independently of the actual cognitive effort of our I. Conversely, the cognitive efforts of our I must proceed lawfully in accordance with the content of our I-consciousness. Within our I, then, real and ideal processes form an inseparable unity. This unity is accessible to immediate experience. Returning to the matter of lies, we come to the conclusion: *a being that knows itself is unable to lie.*

We should envision the angels as beings who always and in everything they do experience the unity of real and ideal processes—a unity which we humans only experience very exceptionally in the awareness of our I. This means that when an angel thinks of a table, a table comes into being. When an actual table enters the field of angelic perception the angels will think of that table only according to its essence and in no other way. For angels always *manifest* their true nature, even when they cognize, just as we humans do when we become aware of our I. To expand on the example of the table: when angels think about a table they *become* the table. And paradoxically, 'seeing' a table for an angel means 'thinking' the table and thereby *creating* it.

In a previous chapter we have identified I-consciousness as the model and archetype of all spiritual-scientific knowledge. The reason is now becoming obvious: our I-awareness is that part of human consciousness which is most angel-like. It opens the way for us to know other spiritual beings beyond ourselves. Even so, we must realize from everything we have discussed so far that the angels' relationship to truth is fundamentally different from ours. *In accordance with their own purely spiritual nature angels live in the truth. Angels cannot lie.*[70]

Angels are in tune with the spirit. At the same time they are connected with human beings. But we humans are incarnated on earth and our nature allows us to be truthful or untruthful by our own choice. Between us and the angels there exists therefore a double interdependence. On the one hand, the angels act as our guardians whose task it is to offer guidance to each individual entrusted to them and help them to live in accordance with the signature of their destiny. As angels experience inside and outside as a unity, they actually *live inside* our human destinies, shaping them, understanding them intimately, utterly dedicated to their care.

Yet it is also human destiny to achieve I-consciousness by our own free choice, individually and universally. This essential aspect of our development is free from all angelic influence. It remains entirely in our own hands. It is an area where our relation of dependency with the angels is actually turned upside down and where the angels are dependent on us. They depend on whether or not we are able to take hold of our freedom. To put it more specifically: our influence over the angels is similar to the effect we have on ourselves when we review, interpret and redeem the events of our past (where, as we know, the angels are also at work, in accordance with the laws of the cosmos).

Thinking of this independence makes us appreciate the immense burden of responsibility that comes with our freedom. We feel the full impact of this state of affairs when we realize that the angels have *absolutely no choice* when it comes to working with the real processes in human destinies. They simply do not have the option of refusing or withdrawing from their appointed task (as they might do if they were capable of experiencing the separation between real and ideal processes). Once we become aware of this enormous responsibility the key question in our relation with the angels is this: Can we connect the real processes that surround us (our destinies, our bodies, the world of nature) with matching ideal processes *responsibly, from within our I*—or not?

If the answer is yes, we can offer the angels a field of action worthy of their spiritual nature. In the opposite case, if for instance we prefer dealing with our destinies, our bodies, or with the natural world on a purely instinctive level, then unbeknownst to ourselves we are forcing the angels into a very uncomfortable position. For an angel, being exposed to the inner world of a person who fails to realize their potential for freedom and does not shine the light of that freedom into their own real processes, is mind-destroying and degrading. In former times, the task of 'shining a light' into our minds was done for us by the angels. In our current era of radical inner freedom the task of self-enlightenment is ours and ours alone.

The problem we have touched on here springs from the fact that for the angels, unlike for humans, inner and outer realities, ideal and real processes, thought and will, consciousness and being, always coincide. Let us illustrate this further with an example from sexual life, a subject which is both current and highly charged. Wolf-Ulrich Klünker offers the following comments in his book, *Die Erwartung der Engel* ('Waiting for angels', as above):

> With such experiences, we find the angels again at the boundary between inner and outer realities. By experiencing sexual desire merely as a 'natural drive', we pin down our angels, as it were,

at the border between elemental and soul realities, preventing their activity within the sphere of our individual I, in the space between inside and outside. Imaginations and actual powers are never spiritually separate for the angels. This is a distinction only we humans are able to make. Thus angels remain tied to the human power field. They have no choice but to go along, even with those forces that originate only from within ourselves. No matter what, angels live by means of elementary powers—regardless of whether we manage to lift those powers into our soul experiences or whether we let them influence our souls from the outside, as it were. In short, angels are found wherever a spiritual reality manifests as a powerful force. This certainly applies to the forces of growth and procreation, at whatever stage in human development.[71]

With sexual experiences we are always negotiating the encounter between an *outer* elementary force (the warming of the blood, physical arousal) and an *inner soul experience* of that same elementary force (the desire for closeness and the wish to become one with our intimate partner). This is just one example from the wide range of angelic activities where our actions affect not only our own condition but that of the angels as well. Rudolf Steiner pointed to this correlation in his 1918 lecture, *What does the angel do in our astral body?*

In this lecture Rudolf Steiner explores the activity of angels within. He opens with a question: 'What are the tasks of the beings of the *angeloi* [angels *SH*], the spiritual beings closest to humans, in the astral body in our current epoch?'[72]

According to Steiner, the astral body is that part of our supersensible organism which forms the basis of our soul life—a 'soul body' as it were, which the soul penetrates through and through. Using the terminology introduced previously in this study, we may say that the astral body, or soul organism, comprises all the *real processes* of human soul life—including those we are conscious of and those that remain buried deep in our unconscious (sympathies and antipathies, instincts, drives, passions, etc).

The angels are connected existentially to the *real soul processes* inside us. The human soul is their field of operation, as it were. Rudolf Steiner gives a highly differentiated picture of these angelic operations:

> It can be seen that the beings from the hierarchy of the *angeloi* create images within the human astral body. This involves individual *angeloi* who have particular tasks linked to each human individual as well as the cooperation of all the *angeloi* ... The angels produce images within the human astral body. We can access these images through a method of thinking that has developed into clairvoyance.[73]

Later on in the lecture, Rudolf Steiner identifies three ideals or goals that belong to the images formed by the angels in the human astral body. These ideals are pursued by the angels on behalf of all humanity: *brotherhood* or fellowship in the economic sphere; *freedom* in the religious sphere; and *spirit-knowledge* in the sphere of science. It is vital for the spiritual communion between angels and humans—and for the future of both the human and the angelic realms—that we should become aware of this aspect of the work of the angels:

> Through the consciousness soul and through conscious thinking activity human beings must come to see just how the angels are preparing the future of humanity.[74]

In 1918 Steiner pointed to dramatic occult developments in the twentieth century. He speaks of the dangers we would face if we failed to wake up to the angelic activity described above. The consequences, he suggests, would play out especially in the realm of sexuality. Alas, from an early-twenty-first-century perspective Steiner's dire predictions appear to have become only too real:

> Should this dangerous situation which I have mentioned become a reality, there is a real risk that a certain kind of instinctive knowledge, which is meant to enter human beings in

connection with the mysteries of birth, conception and sexual life as a whole, may potentially become very harmful indeed on account of certain angels who would undergo a special kind of transformation. I am not at liberty to describe this kind of transformation at present because it is part of the higher secrets of initiation science which may not yet be disclosed. One thing I *can* say, however: Within the overall development of humanity it might well come to pass that certain instincts related to sexual life and to sexuality in general, instead of arising in a beneficial way in full waking consciousness, may arise in a harmful and destructive way. Such instincts would not just take the form of sexual aberrations but they would extend their influence into social life, creating new configurations within the body social. Most of all, through the effect of what enters the human blood as a consequence of sexual life, these instincts would cause humans not only to abandon the development of brotherhood on earth but also to actively oppose and rebel against all brotherhood generally. All this would manifest on an instinctual level.[75]

Sexual energies can be enormously powerful. They are, after all, the forces that support the propagation of our species. At the same time, we experience these forces very individually, on the soul level, as drives and desires and as sexual love. On the one hand, then, sexual forces are *effective* according to the laws of the cosmos in the cycle of procreation, from begetting and conceiving to child bearing and birth-giving. On the other hand, we experience these forces as related to *instinctual drives* and, as such, bound up with physical desire and sexual appetite. In the course of the twentieth century, new methods of birth control have made it possible to develop the realm of sexuality as an end in itself in pursuit of sexual self-realization. Given the tension between these two poles of experience, how can sexuality best be individualized to become an expression of our *full humanity*?[76] That, it seems, is one of the great questions asked by the angels today.

The question takes on urgency when we recall how much, in the course of the twentieth century, our public life has been sexualized through commercial advertisements, magazines and films. Commodified sexuality is ubiquitous. It is easy to see that such developments are making it harder for people to have authentic encounters where sexuality expresses genuine tenderness and love. Certainly, the elemental sexual forces that are stirring deep inside us must not be denied—but some of the current trends seem very much tilted to one side and are pushing in the wrong direction.

If, however, we choose a different direction and allow our sexual experiences to be filled with I-consciousness, a new reality can emerge—a chance for our free conscious *striving* for selfhood and our *loving*, freely given to our beloved, to join together. United they begin the work of ennobling our elemental sexual forces, helping us to encounter each other as true individuals.

Rudolf Steiner's reticence to disclose 'at present' (in 1918) the exact nature of the spiritual harm caused by base human instincts makes for unsettling reading. In our own time, the early twenty-first century, we must consider the sobering possibility that what Steiner predicted may already have happened and become historic reality. When we are spiritually asleep and miss out on the impulses from the angelic world, the angels are forced to dwell in raw, darkened real processes, unredeemed by the ideal processes that are mediated by the human I. It is the nature of the angels to live in the unity of real and ideal processes. It is not in their nature to live only with unredeemed instinctual sexual forces. Forcing them to do so pushes them into denying their own spiritual nature. To put it another way, *the angels are forced by human beings to lie. Consequently, they lose their attunement with their own spiritual nature, thereby turning into demonic beings.*

When confronted with such developments it is no use wringing our hands or reaching for the moral high ground.

We must keep in mind that there are many nuances and intermediary forms in the relations between a person and their angel. All we can do is keep being alert, probing our own spiritual situation with great vigilance, and making every effort to take positive steps towards our future in the full awareness of our conscious I.

13. On the destiny of thinking and the relation between angels and humans

So far we have introduced and explored various different stages within the practice of thinking. Let us review these stages once more and push our exploration a bit further. We started out with *ordinary thinking* which, for the most part, uses mental images or representations. On this level we are literally *confronted* with certain representational contents in our mind. Hence this stage is also referred to as *object consciousness*. Object consciousness is what we normally use in everyday life. Percepts and concepts are mixed together completely.

The next stage involves *pure thinking* which we have discussed at some length. Pure thinking requires far greater effort from the thinker than ordinary representational thought. It operates exclusively among purely conceptual relations. These do not arise spontaneously in our consciousness. We have to produce them by our own efforts. On the other hand, the *content* in pure thinking is not created by the thinker. The contents of pure thought rest in themselves and obey their own laws. The thinker merely becomes aware of their lawful structure. It takes serious discipline and sustained practice to develop pure thinking as a skill. We have described how by means of such practice we are able to develop pure thinking into an organ for *clairvoyant thinking* (see the chapter, 'On pure thinking').

Awareness of our I opens up an existential dimension in pure thinking. As we make progress in the practice of meditation and pure thinking our I-consciousness grows ever stronger and richer in inner substance. In the chapter, 'Angelic encounters and spiritual-scientific investigation', we explained how to move to a new and creative level of thinking and to unknown modes of being. *Living thinking,* the next level of noetic activity, reveals itself little by little. It enables us to discover new spiritual qualities within our sense perceptions, our feelings and our will impulses, and to take these new qualities into our inner being.

Reflecting on these various metamorphoses we may ultimately look upon thinking itself as an evolutionary process with its own destiny—the 'destiny of thinking'. In order to have their own supersensible experiences, it is vital for anthroposophical spiritual researchers to participate in the destiny of thinking. Let us look at an excerpt from a text by Rudolf Steiner where this topic is dealt with at some length. The excerpt is taken from a short pamphlet, *Cosmology, Religion, and Philosophy* (1922) where Steiner discusses the different stages of thinking from an archetypal point of view.

> [By strengthening our thinking through meditative practice] we will be able to access first of all the thinking aspect of higher consciousness. But in this we will not succeed without first having let go of thinking. Successful meditation leads us towards experiencing a release from thinking. To begin with, we ground ourselves in our essential being. Then a certain undefined inner experience can arise—but we are not strong enough to grasp this new inner state with our thoughts. The capacity to do so will grow little by little. Our inner activity increases and the strength of our thinking is fired up, albeit from a totally different source than is the case in our ordinary consciousness. In ordinary consciousness we only experience ourselves in the present moment. But when through sustained soul practice our thinking is kindled in a new way, having gone through non-thinking and having arrived at Imagination, we begin to experience the events of our entire lifespan, from birth until now, as our own 'I'. Memories from our ordinary consciousness are experienced in a somewhat similar way. These are mental images that are experienced in the present moment. They only really relate to the past by virtue of their content. At first, when we begin to have Imaginations, such memories recede. We then begin to view the past as if it was present now. Ordinarily, when we use our physical senses our attention is directed to things as we see them arranged next to each other in space. Likewise, during Imagination we direct our awakened soul

activity towards the various events of our life. The whole temporal succession of events then appears before us as a simultaneous unit. The whole arc of our becoming manifests as a now.[77]

It may come as a surprise that Rudolf Steiner should advocate for a 'release of thinking', as he does in this passage. Yet it is true: the training of thinking can only lead to higher forms of consciousness if we learn to let go of our ordinary thought processes for a time. That is to say, as our thinking develops it must progress until it reaches a certain limit or borderline at which it is lost. Our thinking then suffers a kind of death and all we are left with is an undefined inner experience of our own inner being. What Rudolf Steiner is describing as 'non-thinking' is a key experience and all too easily overlooked. Ordinary ways of approaching knowledge, including those familiar from mainstream science, are intensely focused on contents, conclusions and results. But being very much fixated on contents is a real obstacle to experiencing non-thinking on the meditative path of knowledge.

How exactly does 'non-thinking' work? At the beginning of our meditation process, before reaching non-thinking, we are focusing on some content in the form of ordinary mental imaging. Once we have reached the level of pure thinking this focus is intensified. Step by step we bring the thought content of our meditation to the greatest possible clarity. At a culmination of that process we *dissolve* the thought, as it were, before our inner eye. This is a moment of *death* in our thinking—but what it leaves behind is an inner experience of pure *strength*. In this strength we can feel our own being. Eventually, going through this state we arrive at what Steiner calls 'Imagination'.

Steiner follows this up by describing yet another very powerful experience: the appearance of all the events of our entire lifespan, from birth to the present moment, in the form of a great tableau. Ordinary memory provides us with images that remind us of the past yet 'are experienced in the present moment'. But as soon as Imagination occurs such memory images disappear from our mind. Our own present *time* is effectively transformed into an imaginative *space* where all the events of our past appear together:

> The whole temporal succession of events then appears before us as a simultaneous unit. The whole arc of our becoming manifests as a now.

A first dawning of this experience is the notion of *destiny imagination* which we introduced in the chapter 'Our guardian angels'. The peculiar way in which events that normally follow each other are experienced in space, next to each other—or rather 'within' each other—marks our entry into the spiritual world. The shift in our relation to time signals our entry in the sphere of the angels.

It is interesting to note that many near-death accounts also include descriptions of such a tableau. We read descriptions of how the whole of life passes before one's inner eye like a movie. The frequent reference to the experience of films shows to what extent supersensible experiences are filtered by prevalent cultural concepts. On reflection, what characterizes the movie experience is precisely that the audience are *separated* from the events on the screen. During its running time we are *physically distant* from the projection while the *illusion* is created of us being immersed in the drama. But this is much more like the experience of ordinary memory than of Imagination. Steiner is very clear that with Imagination we do not 'merely experience memory pictures of our life'. Rather, we encounter *thought forms* that are 'condensed into forces of growth'.[78] When we experience Imagination we achieve a vision of the ether body, or life body, in Steiner's terminology.

Just as we approach such threshold events we may experience a certain doubt: when we begin to have spiritual experiences should we not first develop a proper *conceptual understanding* of how time is re-polarized, as Rudolf Steiner describes it? Yes indeed, conceptualizing our spiritual experiences is important because it allows us to form *appropriate judgements* [German: *entsprechend qualifiziert*] about them. Using the terms of our theory of knowledge we may say: In order to experience total reality, we must bring together our spiritual experiences and their corresponding concepts.

*

We can now distinguish four stages of thinking:

- ordinary thinking in mental images;
- pure thinking;
- non-thinking / the experience of forces alone;
- Imagination / living thinking.

Going through these four stages in a conscious way means experiencing and co-creating the *destiny of thinking* within our own mind. The ability to move freely and consciously among the various stages and their transitions is a fundamental requirement of anthroposophical research. By devoting ourselves to meditative thinking and giving ourselves wholeheartedly to the forces that lie hidden within we can gradually form our thinking into a 'spiritual eye'. Rudolf Steiner describes this process at the beginning of *Cosmology, Religion, and Philosophy*:

> Just as mathematicians 'see' equations in their mind's eye, so spiritual researchers see with their 'spiritual eye'. At first, all efforts and methods of spiritual researchers are aimed at building their own 'spiritual organs'. Once their 'science' is well embedded in these organs, the spiritual world will open up and spread before the seeker. Those who do research in the world of the senses are directing their scientific efforts *outwards*, towards results and solutions. Those who search for the spirit use the practice of science only as a preparation for *inner vision*. By the time the vision arises the task of science must already be accomplished. If 'clairvoyance' means receiving visions then what the spiritual researcher does may be called 'exact clairvoyance'.[79]

Evidently, this 'exact clairvoyance' requires careful preparation in order to gradually transform our thinking into a 'spiritual eye'. Since the development of thinking is about joining together content and power—power becoming the conscious content of thought and contents turning into creative thought power—its outcome involves entering the sphere of the angels. For, as we recall, the content and the power of thinking always coincide for the angels. This is the path towards communicating consciously with our guardian angel. Meeting the angels with a spiritual 'habitus' that harmonizes with their being draws us closer to them. It seems obvious that shining our inner light towards the angels would prompt a response in kind, allowing the angels to act according to their inner nature while developing their own potential too. If we didn't kindle that inner light we would remain spiritually blind and mute, as it were, and the angels would find few contact points to integrate harmoniously with our being. This can cause them to become perverted and demonic, as we have mentioned in the previous chapter.

It has been our overall goal all along to provide readers with material that helps develop their 'spiritual eye'. In particular, we worked with the concept of substance and discussed some of its more subtle applications in I-consciousness and the knowledge of angels. If the practice of directing life choices from our I is well established over a long period of time we may have a very curious experience. This experience does not arise from study or meditation per se but rather from giving ourselves wholeheartedly to the events and circumstances of our lives. We may feel that all our meditative efforts are beginning to dissipate more and more until they appear to *dissolve*, as it were. We begin to wonder where our meditative progress disappears to in the midst of the hustle and bustle of life or the latest calamity. At such moments we feel very keenly the loss of all the spiritual clarity and strength we had worked so hard to achieve. But then, delving more deeply into our sense of loss, we may see another, sharply contrasted feeling rise to the surface. Perhaps we can capture this 'complementary' feeling best by summing up everything about our inner growth, our spiritual insights and our new capacities, in a single expression, the 'Word' and declare: *The Word dies and becomes life.* Or put differently: *The Word strives to become life and strength.*

The process evoked in these words can only begin once we *let go* of our meditative efforts. Our spiritual striving can then begin to blend into the circumstances of our lives. At first this happens quite unconsciously. Only *with hindsight* are we able to listen for echoes and resonances and realize what has become of our efforts—what has become of us. Perhaps this makes us wonder: Does our spiritual work actually *carry* us while we lead our lives—or not?

Experiencing how the Word is dissolved is like experiencing a death. But when the Word first becomes active in our lives it is like a birth: something new is coming to life. This birth process can manifest in very simple everyday situations. For example, while meeting with another person it may happen that we suddenly see this person in a totally new light, as if for the first time. Or we may listen to someone talking and all of a sudden become aware that our listening has led us deep into the other's being. The other person is *speaking their truth inside us.* Again, we may be taking a walk outside when a sudden realization flashes up inside and stirs us with a kind of elemental power: 'I am touching the earth while the spirit of my I is carrying my body through space.' What all these examples have in common is a kind of instantaneous fulguration, a spiritual presencing, intense, unprompted and utterly unexpected. We may compare this to the intensity with which children experience new discoveries. We need to nourish and fine-tune our sensibilities so as not to miss these moments of presencing and their connection to our meditative work.

If we realize how closely such moments of childlike intensity relate to our meditative efforts, and if we are able to shed light on those experiences and express them in ideas, concepts and words, we reach through to what is expressed in the phrase, *Life condenses again into the Word.* Thus we have come full circle, having experienced the entire process as a rhythmic wholeness: *The Word dies and becomes Life. Life dies and becomes a new Word.*

The double

What we have just described is a process by which our soul becomes more and more childlike. But other experiences awaken too and spring up in the soul. Our shadow side begins to stir and wants to express itself. Images rise from the depth of the soul bearing hate, anger, violence, and the will to dominate. The soul is attacked with sudden assaults. These are, as it were, the 'counter-images' of humanity. Their power is fearsome. They can coerce the soul, persuade it to nurture the most intensely negative feelings. And they can push the soul into taking aggressive actions against others. The 'counter-images' embody the opposite of humanness and act against all the ideals and aspirations we have formed in inner freedom. For the counter-images themselves are not brought forth in freedom. On the contrary, the soul feels invaded, possessed, defiled and violated by them. Even if their attacks can seem like those of an outside agent we are forced to acknowledge that these images very much belong to our own being. Then we must ask ourselves: Are we spiritually strong enough to allow such images into the ambit of our consciousness without being overwhelmed by them?

We know that the shadows of the soul cannot be pushed away. Our dark side does not define us but it still belong to us existentially. We must engage with our shadows and try to transform them. In certain spiritual traditions the soul's shadow is referred to as the *double*, or doppelganger. Rudolf Steiner also calls it the *guardian of the threshold*. The appearance of the guardian of the threshold marks a moment of crisis, a threshold situation, as the soul is confronted with the evil that lives within it. On the one hand, it is a hallmark of this particular threshold situation that the evil and cruelty we bear in ourselves takes the appearance of an independent character, an opponent. This helps create a certain distance between us and our opponent. On the other hand, the power of the negative images forces us to recognize *ourselves* in the double—an extremely painful and sobering experience.

Let us visualize the human being standing between their double and their guardian angel. Both the double and the angel are sources of power with strong effects on the soul. But these effects can be lessened and eventually brought to peace through our human freedom—more especially through the freedom we experience in our thinking. Based on that freedom, fully aware of both the double and the angel, we are capable of initiating the moral impulses that build up our core being. Most importantly, we must meet both our angel and our double at 'eye level'. Failing to do so runs the risk of causing a kind of spiritual short circuit between our double and our angel. Such an unwholesome connection would remain below the threshold of consciousness and turn us into a helpless plaything of forces we neither understand nor recognize.[80]

In this chapter we have described a wide range of experiences, including moments of heightened spiritual awareness and disturbing visions of the evil within us. Such experiences are inevitable when our thinking matures into a 'spiritual eye'. They are the Imaginations and Inspirations of our own guardian angel and our double. However, far more important than having this or that experience is reaching a fundamental *understanding* of our experiences. In these pages we have worked our way towards such an understanding. Only true insight and understanding enable us to hold our own against the dangers of dark insinuations and of sentimentality in our spiritual life. Thus strengthened we may meet the threshold in freedom and consciousness, standing with confidence and poise between our double and our angel.

14. Meditative epilogue: In conversation with the angels

At the end of our study we invite the reader to envision a kind of conversation between humans and angels, using thought as an artistic medium, as it were. We shall revisit ideas we have developed, elaborated or hinted at earlier—this time in the form of conceptual Imaginations. We shall try and create a more comprehensive tableau of all those connections and correlations which, until now, we have only expressed through abstract definitions. By its very nature our meditative thought process will be open-ended and without predetermined outcome. First, we follow our established method and engage our subject in a spiritual-scientific way. Next, we raise our reflections to a higher state of spiritual-poetic concentration. Following that, we wait patiently for the fruits of our efforts to reveal themselves. It is vital to have the patience and allow our meditation to resonate in its own time. Experience teaches us that only time and inner distance produce results of real spiritual-scientific value.

The steps we have just outlined fit into a very definite historical context. Speaking generally, our project is to renew and expand the Aristotelian scientific method by bringing it together with Platonic imagination and vision. That is to say, we are moving from *pure thinking* towards *imaginative thinking*. John Scotus Eriugena, whose writings we have encountered previously, has taken very definite steps in this direction in his great work, *Periphyseon (On the Division of Nature)*. Eriugena observes:

> Not only is the angelic nature established in the human but also the human is established in the angelic. For it is created in everything of which the pure intellect has the most perfect knowledge and becomes one with it. ... Moreover the angel is made in man, through the understanding of angel which is in man, and man is in the angel through the understanding of man which is established in the angel.[81]

At first we may be inclined to regard such statements as mere fantasy. If, however, we take Eriugena's thoughts at face value we can make certain discoveries about our own mental process. One thing we discover is the phenomenon of inner *evidence*, i.e. of direct insight into complex thought connections (see our chapter 'On pure thinking'). When experiencing *evidence* the eye of the mind beholds the totality of a conceptional nexus and all its implications with perfect clarity. Our thoughts exist within and through our thinking activity and, conversely, our thinking activity exists within and through our thoughts. If we transpose this scenario to thinking about angels, we find that the same mutual relationship also exists between us as thinkers and the 'angels as concept'. We are then able to link 'angels as a concept' with specific supersensible perceptions or feelings we have encountered in meditation. By way of example, let us look at Eriugena's quasi-meditative verse sequence regarding the relation between humans and angels:

Affirmation of human beings:

Humans are rational mortal beings endowed with a soul.

Negation of angels:

Angels are *not* rational mortal beings endowed with a soul.

Negation of human beings:

Humans are *not* rational mortal beings endowed with a soul.

Affirmation of angels:

Angels are rational mortal beings endowed with a soul.

These four statements can produce four more by being reversed.[82]

The four headings—some of which are in direct logical contradiction with one another—adds considerable depth to the concept of angels. They expand our thinking by setting off a kind of inner rhythmic motion that generates more ideas. How does this come about? Let us look more closely at each of Eriugena's lines.

Affirmation of human beings. The first line can be interpreted as, 'Human beings are *thinking themselves* as human beings', meaning: we are thinking of ourselves as a 'rational mortal beings endowed with a soul'. In response to this, the second heading announces the *Negation of angels* (line three). Angels are indeed '*not* mortal beings endowed with a soul'. The second heading could also be interpreted as, 'angels are *thinking themselves* as angelic beings'. For angels know their own nature by becoming aware of their differences with humans, especially differences in the way we know ourselves. According to the philosopher Hegel, 'negation' can mean three different things: *denial, preservation* and *transcendence.* Indeed, affirming humanity *denies* angelic nature in a certain way. Yet it also defines and *preserves* the angels by highlighting their differences from us humans, as we have suggested. And finally, the angels *transcend* our humanity because they are immortal beings and their nature is both above and beyond ours.[83]

The third headline, *Negation of human beings* (line five), applies when humans move from thinking only themselves to conceiving the thought of angels. 'Human beings are thinking angelic beings' means bringing to awareness the angelic nature within ourselves. In that case, we become more than just 'rational mortal beings endowed with souls'. Also, the fourth and last heading pronounces the *Affirmation of angels* (line seven) which we may interpret as 'angels are thinking human beings'—meaning: 'the angelic nature within us'. In the process of thinking humans the angels are confronted with our mortality. In this sense the angels really are 'rational mortal beings endowed with souls' within us.

In light of the above, let us try and rephrase the four sections of Eriugena's verse somewhat freely:

Affirmation of human beings:

Humans are thinking themselves as human beings. (4)

Negation of angels:

Angels are thinking themselves as angelic beings. (3)

Negation of human beings:

Human beings are thinking angelic beings. (2)

Affirmation of angels:

Angels are thinking human beings, i.e. the angelic nature within us. (1)

Eriugena observes that 'four more' statements can be produced if the first set is 'reversed'. What he means becomes obvious when we read the four new statements above from bottom to top instead of top to bottom (i.e. (1) to (4)).

Meditating on the various levels of meaning in Eriugena's four verses we are entering a kind of rhythmical life, a rhythmic pulsing of the mind. The relationship between our mind and the mind of angels becomes vivid and real. The intellectual meaning of those eight lines becomes less important than experiencing the power of the dance and the jostle between them. By meditating on such material regularly we lift ourselves little by little out of our ordinary object consciousness. We are moving toward *process consciousness* and are entering a spiritual state that has a kind of *musical quality*. We begin to live within the power of our self-generated thought currents. Our thinking becomes a light that shines not only in our mind but also our etheric body, our life functions. We may even have the sensation that the light of our thinking moves and circulates through our head, neck and chest, touching and illuminating the different chakras associated with those areas.

*

When we experience thinking as a flow of *power* it is revealed as a manifestation of *will forces*. A whole new dimension opens to us once we begin experiencing thinking as a force of will within the body. We become aware how the 'inner human being' inhabits the physical body. The hard boundaries of our skull and skin and bones dissolve and expand, as it were. They form a new periphery around us. Within this new surround our thoughts live as currents, impulses and gestures.

Yet our thinking lives not only in the periphery of our cranium. It draws power from the lower regions of the body too. This raises an important question: How is the life of our thinking differentiated within our bodily organism, particularly in the regions of the head, throat and heart?

Observing the pathways of our thinking from the head downwards is not a simple task. When exploring the question during meditation we should distinguish two levels of experience: the level of content and the level of general human experience [German: *Menschenkundliches*]. With respect to content, as our thinking becomes more and more agile we eventually come to experience thinking as pure movement. We are given the impression of inwardly sculpting our thoughts. From the point of view of a spiritual physiology, the central spot where we normally locate our thinking begins to shift. Ordinary thinking (and to some extent pure thinking) is usually experienced inside our head, or at any rate related to the head. Living thinking, on the other hand, lights up in the periphery of the head and develops dynamic forces that stream downwards into our organism. To follow this process consciously is exceedingly difficult. We encounter our own organism as something ready-made, as it were—yet our meditation changes both ourselves and our body. We learn from this that universal insights about human experiences [*Menschenkundliches*] can only obtain as new conditions are being created within our own organism. Bearing this in mind, we may choose to shift the focus of our meditation to the task of releasing our thinking from being tied to the head and allowing it to engage with the processes that live in the throat and heart.[84]

The head, with the brain as a thinking organ, forms our thoughts by acting as a kind of mirror for spiritual realities. The throat enables us to speak our thoughts. And in the heart feelings are kindled that relate to those thoughts and words. On one level, the three areas are quite distinct, both physiologically (head, throat and heart) and on the level of the soul (thoughts, words and feelings). Their connections and the interactions between them happen on an unconscious level. But the encounter with our guardian angel suggests that new relations between our thoughts, words, and feelings are possible—relations we can forge for ourselves in conscious freedom. It seems as though the angels are teaching us, nudging us to make the most of our quest for knowledge, for the sake of our destiny in body, soul and spirit—until one day we ourselves become free bearers of the Word.

***

At the end our of study we share some further material for meditative practice, especially intended for those who wish to begin a conversation with their guardian angel.

We humans are fallible.
We humans are capable of lying.
We humans are capable of striving for the truth (or the opposite).

The angels are infallible.
The angels are incapable of lying.
The angels are incapable of striving for the truth (or the opposite).

We humans are free to form our own relationship to truth.
The angels live in truth by their own spiritual nature.

Free, fallible humans are united in a community of being with the angels who live in truth by their own spiritual nature.

When angels take us humans into their thoughts they become our destiny.
When we humans take angels into our thoughts we become like the angels and an angelic being emerges within us.

Thus the angels become our destiny and we become the destiny of angels.

When we become like the angels the angels' destiny is changed. When we take hold of the power of our guardian angel we release our angel to develop further. We show our guardian angel how inner strength can transform error into truth. This opens up a new experience for the angels which fills them with human-like enthusiasm: that it is possible to relate to truth on the basis of freedom.

We enter into the sphere of the angels by stepping through the portal of time and by learning to behold the stream of time beyond all transience. On the path towards the spirit the glance of our inner eye is changed into an angelic glance and the angelic glance into a human one.

Our guardian angel teaches us that our search for knowledge can shape our body and our destiny. Thus the angel speaks: 'Your words, O human being, must die and become life. Your words crave to enter the stream of life in power.' Every angel eagerly awaits the moment when they can reveal to the person entrusted to them how such a process unfolds in the human organism and in human destiny.

Always standing by us, the guardian angel ponders thus: 'O earthly human being, learn to see the past in the light of the future. Then my power will lead you from suffering to creating your destiny. Take hold of my angelic power, O human being, and pour it forth into the conduct of your life and into the many-layered sheaths of your body. When angelic power enlivens the human senses, the destinies of human beings will begin to intertwine and be penetrated through and through with light and warmth.'

Thanks to us humans, the angels can share in the experience of freedom. We experience freedom in our search for truth. The angels live in the truth by their spirit-nature. But human freedom can affect the nature of angels and their relation to truth. By the power of our guardian angels we humans can form a new relationship to our bodily sheaths. Equally, by our own free deeds the angels can receive the gift of new experiences into their truth-filled bodies.

Freedom and devotion to the truth among humans are the new breath, the new cosmic foundation allowing all spiritual beings to grow and evolve.

Reflections on the cover art

Shall we compare the human being to a keyhole through which we catch a glimpse of another, truer world? On the other side of that keyhole all beings reveal their true nature.

Only when we look through our own keyhole do we know ourselves, our I. There, in the soul-spiritual realm beyond the physical world, we find our angel companion. S/he is our spiritual You.

Angels listen with the ears of the heart. Their companionship reflects back to us everything we think, feel and do. Even though angels are fundamentally connected to the *sun*, what they do when they accompany us with their steady gaze feels rather more like a *moon* gesture. Of course, the angels shine with a far greater light than we do, being older and spiritually more advanced. But in their dedication to humble service they lower themselves to receive, moon-like, the fledgling light of our sun-born freedom.

Our true self is hovering far above us—too far to catch more than a small glimpse of it through that keyhole. The loftiest part of us is also the most childlike, always created anew, forever alive. Our guardian angel is keeping safe for us those things we cannot yet carry by ourselves. Halfway between us and our guardian angel, that's where we find our own inner child. It is our inner sun, shining overhead.

We have only one guardian angel. But our shadow escort has many faces.

No angel is like another. Each person's double is unique. So are the many ways the shadow forces play into each other. The double has both luciferic and ahrimanic qualities. Our luciferic double indulges deliciously in our meditations, our prayers, our love-making. The ahrimanic double is aroused by our fears. Our connection with Ahriman is established when we first become aware that death is part of our reality. Both conspire to paint that anxious, fearsome look on our face: 'Woe is me, what have I done?…' These beings and others besides are the worms inside our soul—the inner dragons, pigs, dogs, roosters, wolves, monkeys, what have you.

To the left of the doppelganger's head we see our life's challenges lurking. Always lying in wait for us. Always something different.

But the angel now—we can trust our guardian! The angel is our anchor overhead, our grounding in the heavens, our link to the world of the stars.

If you look at the threefold double in the picture and see it as *one* creature with sexual appendages, then perhaps you are looking at it through your own double. But it is hard to tell, the double being a shadow figure….

A light shines upon us, coming from the angel and from our higher being. The shadow we cast is following us, dragging us along with all those untransformed, unredeemed experiences of ours. Such is the double. But our own light is constantly being reborn within our inner, childlike, higher selves. Our guardian angel never tires of observing, preserving, protecting and nurturing that inner child of ours—or of talking about us to his/her fellow angels. … Such a precious thing!

The cover image I have created was inspired by the following passage in Steffen's book:

> This birth process can manifest in very simple everyday situations. For example, while meeting with another person it may happen that we suddenly see this person in a totally new light, as if for the first time. Or we may listen to someone talking and all of a sudden become aware that our listening has led us deep into the other's being. The other person is *speaking their truth inside us.* Again, we may be taking a walk outside when a sudden realization flashes up inside us and stirs us with a kind of elemental power: 'I am touching the earth while the spirit of my I is carrying my body through space.' What all these examples have in common is a kind of instantaneous fulguration, a spiritual presencing,

intense, unprompted and utterly unexpected. We may compare this to the intensity with which children experience new discoveries. We need to nourish and fine-tune our sensibilities so as not to miss these moments of presencing and their connection to our meditative work. ... What we have just described is a process by which our soul becomes more and more childlike. But other experiences awaken and spring up in the soul. Our shadow side begins to stir and wants to express itself.

Johannes Greiner

Note about the new edition

This book was first published on Michaelmas 2004 in a private edition entitled *Wesen und Erscheinung. Zugleich ein Versuch, Mensch und Engel zu denken* ('On Being and Appearance: Exploring the conceptual dimensions of humans and angels'). That work had been made possible by a research grant from the Anthroposophical Society in 2003 and 2004, under the guidance of Wolf-Ulrich Klünker and Gottfried Stockmar. In addition, I enjoyed many stimulating and productive conversations with my friend Heidjer Reetz. The new edition contains a number of changes in wording and some clarifications. The basic argument and structure of the original are unchanged.

Notes

1   Aristotle, *Metaphysics* 1031a, transl. W. D. Ross, in: Jonathan Barnes
    (ed.), *The Complete Works of Aristotle. The Revised Oxford Translation*.
    Vol. 2. Bollingen Series LXXI:2. Princeton, New Jersey: Princeton
    University Press, 1984, p.1628. [*SH* quotes from the German trans-
    lation by Adolf Lasson, Jena (1907). *FL*]
2   Aristotle, *Metaphysics* 1031b, Barnes 2, p.1628.
3   By way of example, we may mention Jostein Saether who, in an
    interview in *Anthroposophy Worldwide* (16-2-2003), states the follow-
    ing about Imagination as a stage of knowledge: 'In my opinion it
    is not so important, in this case, to gain immediate certainty about
    our experiences. We always seek for certainty and full possession of
    everything. But it is uncertain whether we can get there as quickly
    as all that. It is important first to develop the stage referred to as
    Imagination. *What is important, in the first place, is that we obtain some
    kind of inner images or supersensible experiences at all.*' (Italics added
    by *SH*.)
4   Aristotle, *Metaphysics* 995a/b, Barnes 2, p.1572-73. [In this quote,
    SH follows a more recent German translation, Hamburg (1995). *FL*]
5   See also my three essays, 'Philosophie und Anthroposophie. Wür-
    digung und Aufgabe eines Aufsatzes Rudolf Steiners', in: *Der
    Europäer*, July/August 2007, October 2007 and February 2008. [Not
    translated. *FL*]
6   Gernot Böhme, *Am Ende des Baconschen Zeitalters*. ('At the End of
    the Age of Bacon.') Frankfurt/Main, 1993, p.151f. [Not translated.
    FL]
7   Böhme, *Am Ende des Baconschen Zeitalters*, p.154.
8   Böhme, *Am Ende des Baconschen Zeitalters*, p.163.
9   Böhme, *Am Ende des Baconschen Zeitalters*, p.163f.
10 Aristotle, *Categories* 2a, transl. J. L. Ackrill, in: Barnes 1, p.4.
    [*Italics* follow Barnes' edition. Readers should be aware that the
    word 'subject' in this quote is an accepted scholarly translation,
    derived from the Latin *subiectum,* of the original Greek *hypokeime-
    non.* In the context of Aristotle's philosophy, the meaning of 'sub-
    ject' is very different from any of its current meanings in English
    (a person, a branch of knowledge, a topic...). The root meaning of
    both *hypokeimenon* and *subiectum* is 'what lies underneath'. For Aris-
    totle it denotes a reality of being which underlies as a 'substrate' the

sensory appearance of physical things and beings as well as words and concepts (*logos*). *Hypokeimenon / subiectum* expresses thus one of the basic ontological assumptions in Aristotle's metaphysics. As a reminder for the reader, we have inserted 'substrate' each time the word 'subject' appears in a quote. *FL*]

11   Aristotle, *Categories* 2b, Barnes 1, p.5.

12   Aristotle, *Categories* 3b, Barnes 1, p.6.

13   Plato, *Republic* 476a, tr. Paul Shorey, in: Edith Hamilton & Huntington Cairns (eds): *The Collected Dialogues of Plato*. Bollingen Series LXXI, Princeton, New Jersey: Princeton University Press, 1961, p.715.

14   Plato, *Republic* 507b, Hamilton & Cairns, p.742.

15   Aristotle expresses the primacy of substances in his own way: 'Further, it is because the primary substances are subjects [substrates] for everything else that they are called substances most strictly.' *Categories* 2b/3a. Barnes 1, p.5.

16   Aristotle, *Categories* 4a, Barnes 1, p.7.

17   Plato, *Republic* 518c, Hamilton & Cairns, p.750f.

18   On 13 November, 2003, the German magazine, *Die Zeit* featured an article entitled 'Intelligenztest für Bestien' ('IQ test for beasts') which gives a summary of the scientific consensus on this question. It includes the following passage from Stephen Budiansky's book, *If a Lion Could Talk. How Animals Think* (London: Phoenix, 1998): 'In fact the most astonishing things (astonishing to us, that is) that animals do almost certainly have nothing whatever to do with conscious thought as *we* know it.' [Budiansky, *If a Lion Could Talk*, p.xviii. *FL*]. As summarized by Michael Miersch, Budiansky concludes that 'humans are qualitatively distinct from animals—from all animals, including chimpanzees. The big difference lies in the appearance of language. Primates can hardly go beyond "Give Coco banana", even after years of training. By contrast, human infants eagerly absorb syntax and semantics and are able to understand complex linguistic structures after only a few months.' [See Budiansky, *If a Lion Could Talk*, 149-153. *FL*] Budiansky states: 'The ability to have thoughts about thoughts, which language gave us, is a discontinuous leap [in evolution].' [Budiansky, *If a Lion Could Talk*, p.190. *FL*]

19   Here we have purposefully given a certain Platonic slant to our line of reasoning.

20 See also Rudolf Steiner, *Anthroposophische Leitsätze* ('Anthroposophical Leading Thoughts') GA 26, Dornach 1989, p.16: 'Ordinary life experience shows the enormous extent to which our mental/spiritual experiences are dependent on the physical body. We become aware that our self-awareness may be lost in the course of ordinary life. This prompts a deeply anxious question: Is there any kind of self-knowledge that goes beyond our ordinary experience and might give us assurance regarding the nature of our true self?'

21 Plato, *Republic* 511 b, Hamilton & Cairns, p.746.

22 The experience of thinking clairvoyance is fundamental for all spiritual research. Hegel gives a description of it in his *Phenomenology of Spirit*: 'When we think we move with objects that are neither images nor forms but rather *concepts*, that is, distinct beings-in-themselves which our mind nevertheless does not spontaneously experience as distinct from itself. As such, images, shapes and beings have the property of being distinct from our consciousness. A concept, on the other hand, is at the same time something that *is*—and this property, insofar as it is part of itself, constitutes its particular content—but at the same time, as this content is also something we cognize, our consciousness remains aware of being one with this definite and distinct being. This is in contrast to the case of mental images where, at first, our mind has to make real efforts before realizing that it is dealing with representations belonging to itself. By contrast, a concept is always our own concept, unmediated by anything else. In thinking we can be free because we are not contained within something else but remain within ourselves absolutely. And the object, which we apprehend as a being, is at the same time our own undivided being-with-ourselves. Thus, our movements within concepts are movements within ourselves.' G. W. F. Hegel, *Phänomenologie des Geistes*, Hamburg 1988, p.137.

23 Aristotle, *Metaphysics* 1062a, Barnes 2, p.1677.

24 In his book *Strukturphänomenologie* (Dornach, 1983), Herbert Witzenmann described thinking very aptly as *bestimmend rückbestimmte Tätigkeit* ('determining retro-determined activity' or 'feedback loop').

25 An article by Georg Kühlewind is rather illuminating in this context: 'Die Gegenwärtigkeit des Geistes im Hellsichtigen Denken' ('Spiritual presence in clairvoyant thinking') in: *Die Drei*, December 1995.

26 See also my article, 'Das Mysterium des reinen Denkens'. ('The mystery of pure thinking.') in: *Das Goetheanum* 26 (June 2003).

27 See *Walter Johannes Stein—Rudolf Steiner. Dokumentation eines wegweisenden Zusammenwirkens.* ('Walter Johannes Stein and Rudolf Steiner. Documents of a groundbreaking collaboration') Dornach: Verlag am Goetheanum, 1985, p.283f.

27a Dionysius Areopagita is an historic personality of the first-century CE, mentioned in Acts 17:34 as a disciple of Paul in Athens. During the medieval period a significant corpus of mystical writings, known as the 'Dionysian corpus', was attributed to Dionysius Areopagita, disciple of the apostle Paul. These writings became deeply influential not only because of their mystical content but because of their assumed apostolic authority. However, in the fifteenth century Lorenzo Valla, the humanist scholar, argued persuasively that the Dionysian corpus could not have been written before the sixth century CE. Since then, the sixth-century neoplatonic author, who has never been identified, is commonly referred to as 'Pseudo-Dionysius'. Lorenzo Valla's discovery was especially consequential since it denied the Dionysian writings any apostolic authenticity, thereby leaving vulnerable the Roman Church's traditional justification of its hierarchical structure, which drew heavily on the parallel between celestial and ecclesiastical hierarchies made in the (Pseudo)-Dionysian corpus. Rudolf Steiner did not dispute Valla's finding but suggested that the esoteric teachings expressed in the Dionysian writings were nonetheless the expression of an authentic apostolic tradition hearkening back to Paul and the historic Dionysius Areopagita, and transmitted through the centuries through a line of initiates before being written down in the sixth century. See Rudolf Steiner, *Foundations of Esotericism*, Lecture 13 (Berlin, 8 October 1905) in GA 93a. The most recent English translation of the Dionysian corpus is Col. Lubheid (ed): *Pseudo-Dionysius. The Complete Works*. New York, Mahwah: Paulist Press, 1987—FL.

28 Up to this point we have used the terms of 'knowing' and 'thinking' interchangeably. In this chapter we begin to differentiate between the two. We now define thinking as one part of the noetic process which must combine with the other part, perception, in order for reality as a whole to become knowable.

29 Hans Erhard Lauer, *Die Wiedergeburt der Erkenntnis* ('The Rebirth of Knowledge'), Freiburg, 1946, p.168.

30 Rudolf Steiner, *Die Philosophie der Freiheit* ('The Philosophy of Free-dom', also translated as 'The Philosophy of Spiritual Activity') GA 4, Dornach 1995, p.92.

31 See my article, 'Gibt es ein unterbewusstes Erkennen? Eine kritische Frage an Herbert Witzenmann.' ('Does subconscious knowl-edge exists? A critical question for Herbert Witzenmann.') in: *Der Europäer*, April 2007.

32 Rudolf Steiner, *Die Philosophie der Freiheit*, p.247f.

33 Rudolf Steiner, *Grundlinien einer Erkenntnistheorie der Goetheschen Weltanschauung.* ('The Science of Knowing. Outline of an Episte-mology Implicit in the Goethean Worldview', previously translated as 'A Theory of Knowledge') GA 2, Dornach, 1999, p.138.

34 Rudolf Steiner repeatedly turned to the question: What is anthropo-sophical spiritual science? For our present purposes, the following definition seems most relevant: 'I conceive of anthroposophy as a scientific investigation of the spiritual world which seeks to avoid the one-sidedness both of science (in so far as it is strictly limited to nature) and of the common sort of mysticism; and which strives, before attempting to penetrate into the spiritual world, to develop first within the searching soul those forces that are active neither in ordinary consciousness nor in ordinary science.' Rudolf Steiner, *Philosophie und Anthroposophie* ('Philosophy and Anthroposophy') GA 35, separate print Dornach 1984, p.5.

35 This and all following quotes are taken from the first edition (Jena, 1794/9) of Fichte's work, *Grundlage der gesamten Wissenschaftslehre* ('Foundations of the Entire Science of Knowledge').

36 'Everyone will hopefully be able to think *themselves.* They will then hopefully realize that in being summoned to this thinking, they are called to something that is very much dependent on their own activ-ity, on *inner activity*, and that, when they achieve what is asked for, they are well and truly affected by their self-activity, that is, by *acting.* They will hopefully be able to distinguish this kind of acting from its *opposite* kind, by which they think objects outside of themselves, and find that in the case of the latter the thinker and the thought are opposites and therefore their activity is aimed at something distinct from themselves, while in the former the thinker and the thought are one and the same, and hence their activity is meant to be directed back onto themselves. They will hopefully understand that—because the thought of themselves can arise in themselves *only*

in this way, since, as they have discovered, the opposite thinking produces a completely different thought in them—they will understand, I say, that the thought of themselves is nothing less than the thought of that action, and the term "I" is nothing beside the designation of this action; and that *I* and *action turned back on itself* are completely identical terms.' J. G. Fichte, *Versuch einer neuen Darstellung der Wissenschaftslehre* (1797/98) ('New attempt of Presenting the Science of Knowledge'), Hamburg 1984, p.42.

37 Rudolf Steiner, *Die Philosophie der Freiheit*, p.109.

38 Rudolf Steiner, *Die Philosophie der Freiheit*, p.109.

39 Plato, *Timaios* 27d, tr. Benjamin Jowett, in Hamilton & Cairns, p.1161.

40 Plato, *Timaios* 29e, Hamilton & Cairns, p.1162.

41 Plato, *Timaios* 28b, Hamilton & Cairns, p.1161.

42 Rudolf Steiner, *Goethes Weltanschauung* ('Goethe's Conception of the World') GA 6, Dornach 1985, p.28.

43 Aristotle, *Categories* 1b-2a, Barnes 1, p.4. [Italics added by *SH*]

44 Aristotle, *Metaphysics* 1017b, Barnes 2, p.1606-7.

45 Rudolf Steiner, *Goethes Weltanschauung*, p.34.

46 Thomas Aquinas, *Treatise on Separate Substances*, Chapter 1.4. [Steffen Hartmann quotes a German translation printed in Wolf-Ulrich Klünker, *Thomas von Aquin: Vom Wesen der Engel* (Stuttgart, 1989), p.21f. The English version printed here follows the bilingual Latin/English edition by Francis J. Lescoe (West Hartford, Connecticut: Saint Joseph College, 1959), edited and html-formatted by Joseph Kenny, O.P., accessible on https://isidore.co/aquinas/SubstSepar.htm. The alternate translation of 'reality' for *veritas* is by Steffen Hartmann. *FL*]

47 Thomas Aquinas, *Treatise on Separate Substances*, 1.4.

48 Thomas Aquinas, *Treatise on Separate Substances*, 1.7.

49 Thomas Aquinas, *Treatise on Separate Substances*, 2.8.

50 Thomas Aquinas, *Treatise on Separate Substances*, 2.8. [Lescoe translates '...since it is not possible to proceed to infinity among movers and things moved...' *FL*]

51 Thomas Aquinas, *Treatise on Separate Substances*, 2.9, 2.10.

52 Thomas Aquinas, *Treatise on Separate Substances*, 2.11, 2.12.

53 Thomas Aquinas, *Treatise on Separate Substances*, 8.41.

54 Thomas Aquinas, *Treatise on Separate Substances*, 8.41.

55 Thomas Aquinas, *Treatise on Separate Substances*, 8.42.

56 Thomas Aquinas, *Treatise on Separate Substances*, Introduction.

57 Thomas Aquinas, *Treatise on Separate Substances*, 17(18).94.

58 Thomas Aquinas, *Treatise on Separate Substances*, 9.48.

59 Thomas Aquinas, *Treatise on Separate Substances*, 9.49.

60 Thomas Aquinas, *Treatise on Separate Substances*, 9.50.

61 Thomas Aquinas, *Treatise on Separate Substances*, 9.51.

62 Rudolf Steiner, *Philosophie und Anthroposophie* ('Philosophy and Anthroposophy') GA 35, Dornach 1984, p.44.

63 Some might object that we are giving too much weight to the *how* of the question instead of the *what*. Many misunderstandings of Rudolf Steiner's thought are caused by just such instances where the *meaning* of a particular passage is very much emphasized without taking into account the *manner* of its presentation. Steiner discusses this difficulty in his lecture, 'The source of artistic imagination and the source of supersensible knowledge': 'That is why it is so important to realize: how the seer expresses something is more significant than what he says. What he says is conditioned by ideas projected from the outside. In order not to appear an utter fool, the seer needs to clothe what he wants to convey in idiomatic sentences and cogent thoughts. In the case of the very highest realms of the spirit it is [particularly] important how the seer expresses himself. We are on the right track when we have understood the reason for the particular way things are expressed; when we have realized that the seer takes great care to speak about some things very briefly, but more at length about others, passing over others in silence; that he always has the need to present a statement first from one point of view, then again from another. It is this kind of creative process that really counts with regard to the higher regions of the spirit world. It is therefore less important for our understanding to listen out for the meaning—which, of course, is still important as a revelation from the spirit world—than to try and move on from the meaning towards the manner in which that meaning is expressed; to sense whether the speaker merely cobbles together various statements and theories or whether he speaks from true experience.' 'Quellen der künstlerischen Phantasie und die Quellen der übersinnlichen Erkenntnis' ('The Sources of Artistic Imagination and the Sources of Supersensible Knowledge', Munich, 5-6 May 1918, in: *Kunst und Kunsterkenntnis* ('Art and Aesthetics') GA 271, Dornach 1991, p.137.

64 John Scotus Eriugena, *Periphyseon* 4, 780B-C, tr. I. P. Sheldon-Williams and John J. O'Meara, in: John O'Meara, *Eriugena: Periphyseon (The Division of Nature)*, Dumbarton Oaks, Washington: Bellarmin, 1987, p.428-29. [Steffen Hartmann quotes after Wolf-Ulrich Klünker, *Johannes Scotus Eriugena—Denken im Gespräch mit dem Engel.* Stuttgart, 1988, p.153. *FL*]

65 Wolf-Ulrich Klünker, *Die Erwartung der Engel* ('Waiting for angels'), Stuttgart 2003, p.100.

66 See also my essay, 'Die Schulung des Denkens und ihre Wirkungen auf die leibliche Organisation' ('The training of thought and its effects on the body'), in: *Die Drei*, December 2005.

67 Original German in: Rainer Maria Rilke, *Gedichte*, Frankfurt: Insel Verlag, 1995, p.629. [English version adapted from the translation of John Waterfield, accessible at http://www.jbeilharz.de. *FL*]

68 This chapter is partly based on insights from Rudolf Steiner's lecture cycle, *Die geistigen Wesenheiten in den Himmelskörpern und Naturreichen* ('Spiritual Beings in the Heavenly Bodies and in the Kingdoms of Nature') GA 136, in particular from lecture three (Helsinki, 5 April, 1912) where Steiner states: 'The way the beings in the next category above us perceive things is very different to our human perceptions. The way human beings perceive is that an outer world approaches them through the senses. They give themselves over to this outside world, as it were. The beings we speak about now do not perceive any outer world through their senses as humans do; instead, their perceptions are similar—I am saying this only by way of analogy—to the kind of perceptions humans have while speaking, for example, or while gesturing with their hands and perceiving their own hand movements, or even while expressing something of their inner life through their facial expressions. Thus, in a certain sense, for the beings that belong to a higher world ... every perception is at the same time a revelation of their own being ... Human beings perceive by losing themselves in the outside world, and they have their own independent inner life by pulling back from the outside world. Those beings that belong to the category just above us... receive revelations instead of perceptions and in these revelations they experience themselves. Instead of an inner life they have the experience of higher spiritual worlds. In short, instead of an inner life they are filled with Spirit. ... Humans are able to perceive something and then to call up quite differ-

ent ideas inside and utter them—ideas that may not correspond at all to their perceptions. This capacity allows human beings to contradict the outer world through lying. This quality ... had to be granted to human beings very particularly in order that they should arrive at the truth by their own free will. ... The beings of the higher category we have discussed here are incapable of this— at least for as long as they keep faith with their own nature. ... If they are to experience themselves at all, these beings must live in the realm of absolute Truth.'

69   Errors and lies have to be distinguished, of course. The former occur unconsciously, the latter carry an intention (though transitions and nuances exist). Most significant for our argument is that the capacities for committing *and* correcting lies and errors are deeply embedded in human nature, and that both are equally linked with our capacity for freedom. They are made possible by the same divide between percept and concept, between reality and consciousness. Furthermore, Rudolf Steiner indicates that the effects of untrue statements on the sixteen-petalled throat chakra are *always* harmful, whether they were made intentionally or unintentionally: 'When we speak or think an untruth we kill off something in the seed of the sixteen-petalled lotus flower. ... If we think or say anything that does not correspond to actual reality, even with supposed best intentions, we destroy a part of our spiritual sense organ. It is the same as with a child who will burn its fingers when it grasps for the fire even though it is done in ignorance.' Rudolf Steiner, *Wie erlangt man Erkenntnisse der höheren Welt?* ('How to Know Higher Worlds') GA 10, p.122.

70   The opposite is true for the fallen angels. They do not have the choice of correcting their errors or mending their ways as humans do. For them, errors and lies are constitutional and inescapable.

71   Wolf-Ulrich Klünker, *Die Erwartung der Engel*, p.77f.

72   Rudolf Steiner, *Der Tod als Lebenswandlung* ('Death as Transformation of Life') GA 182, Dornach 1986, p.142.

73   Rudolf Steiner, *Der Tod als Lebenswandlung*, p.144.

74   Rudolf Steiner, *Der Tod als Lebenswandlung*, p.147f.

75   Rudolf Steiner, *Der Tod als Lebenswandlung*, p.154.

76   On this question see the thoughtful article by Henning Köhler, 'Wie kann Sexualität menschlich werden?' in: *Erziehungskunst*, June 1998.

77   Rudolf Steiner, *Kosmologie, Religion und Philosophie* ('Cosmology, Religion, and Philosophy') GA 25, 1991, p.136f.

78   Rudolf Steiner, *Kosmologie, Religion und Philosophie*, p.100.

79   Rudolf Steiner, *Kosmologie, Religion und Philosophie*, p.82.

80   See also my article, 'Zwischen Ungeduld und Lässigkeit. Von der Schwellensituation im Schaffen Franz Kafkas' ('Between impatience and indolence. Threshold situations in the works of Franz Kafka') in: *Das Goetheanum* 41, 11 October 1998.

81   John Scotus Eriugena, *Periphyseon* 4, 780A-B, O'Meara p.428. [The German version quoted by *SH* is taken from Wolf-Ulrich Klünker, *Johannes Scotus Eriugena*, p.151f and offers a slightly different reading. *FL*]

82   John Scotus Eriugena, *Periphyseon* 1, 444B, O'Meara p.28. [In the original passage of *Periphyseon* the four statements are not presented in verse form but embedded in a prose section discussing the second mode of being and not being: 'Thus, the affirmation of "man" (I mean, man while still in his mortal state) is the negation of "angel", while the negation of "man" is the affirmation of "angel" and vice versa. For if man is a rational, mortal, risible animal, then an angel is certainly neither a rational animal nor mortal nor risible.' The verse format, though germane to the original, was first presented in Wolf-Ulrich Klünker, *Johannes Scotus Eriugena*, p.163. Klünker also appears to expand on Eriugena's thought by adding two lines (6 and 8) which are not traceable in *Periphyseon*. *FL*]

83   On this aspect, see also Wolf-Ulrich Klünker's thoughtful comments about Eriugena's verse (*Johannes Scotus Eriugena*, p.162ff).

84   From the perspective of anthroposophical research, this spiritual-physiological thinking path raises the question of the nature of the human heart. Peter Selg has published a very considerable collection of materials on this topic: *Mysterium cordis: Von der Mysterienstätte des Menschenherzens. Studien zu einer sakramentalen Physiologie des Menschenherzens*. Dornach, 2003, (*The Mystery of the Heart. The Sacramental Physiology of the Heart in Aristotle, Thomas Aquinas, and Rudolf Steiner*. SteinerBooks, 2012). In this book, the author compares various teachings on the heart found in the writings of Aristotle, Thomas Aquinas and Rudolf Steiner. For example, we read on p.92f [p.69f of the English edition]: 'Thomas repeatedly pointed out that the heart is related to the higher cognitive activities, which take place after sensory perception and the development of imaginative

images. He spoke of the "word of the heart" (*verbum cordis*), by no means only in a metaphorical sense. This "word" is the result of the other activities. ... According to Thomas (quoting John of Damascus in this matter), the word that results from this conceptual work of perception is "uttered inventively in the heart" (*in corde pronunciatur*). This concept, necessarily general, serves as the final segment in the process of sensory perception. For Thomas, it was merely the beginning (*principium*) and the tool for the spiritual and intellectual activity of thought. This thought process takes place in the individual penetration and unification of the act of perceiving with what is being perceived. This leads, in the end, to the formation of the word. This is a spiritual conception process in which the spiritual and intellectual forces of thinking and willing in the human being are united in the very center of our being.'

A note from the publisher

For more than a quarter of a century, **Temple Lodge Publishing** has made available new thought, ideas and research in the field of spiritual science.

Anthroposophy, as founded by Rudolf Steiner (1861-1925), is commonly known today through its practical applications, principally in education (Steiner-Waldorf schools) and agriculture (biodynamic food and wine). But behind this outer activity stands the core discipline of spiritual science, which continues to be developed and updated. True science can never be static and anthroposophy is living knowledge.

Our list features some of the best contemporary spiritual-scientific work available today, as well as introductory titles. So, visit us online at **www.templelodge.com** and join our emailing list for news on new titles.

If you feel like supporting our work, you can do so by buying our books or making a direct donation (we are a non-profit/ charitable organisation).

office@templelodge.com

TEMPLE LODGE

For the finest books of Science and Spirit